# The Alphabet Game

# The Alphabet Game

# a bpNichol reader

edited by
Darren Wershler-Henry and Lori Emerson

COACH HOUSE BOOKS, TORONTO

first edition

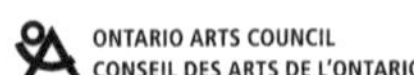


Canadä

Published with the generous assistance of the Canada Council for the Arts and the Ontario Arts Council. Coach House also acknowledges the support of the Government of Canada through the Book Publishing Industry Development Program.

LIBRARY AND ARCHIVES CANADA CATALOGUING IN PUBLICATION

Nichol, b. p., 1944–1988
The alphabet game: a bpNichol reader / bpNichol; edited by Lori Emerson and Darren Wershler-Henry.

ISBN 978-1-55245-187-8

I. Emerson, Lori
II. Wershler-Henry, Darren S. (Darren Sean), 1966–
III. Title.

PS8527.I32A75 2007 C811'.54 C2007-905767-5

drop this jiggerypokery and talk straight turkey meet to mate, for while the ear, be we mikealls or nicholists, may sometimes be inclined to believe others the eye, whether browned or nolensed, find it devilish hard now and again even to believe itself.

– James Joyce, *Finnegans Wake*

# Contents

love • zygal • art facts

THE
COMPLETE
WORKS

bpNichol

§ " # $ % _ & ' ( ) * +
ò 2 3 4 5 6 7 8 9 0 - =

Q W E R T Y U I O P ?
q w e r t y u i o p /

A S D F G H J K L : ^
a s d f g h j k l ; `

Z X C V B N M , . ç
z x c v b n m , . é

---

* any possible permutation
of all listed elements

# concrete and visual poetry

NOT WHAT THE SIREN SANG
BUT WHAT THE FRAG  MENT          for margaret avi

---

leaf    autumn    sky
flea    umantu    kys
over  an  over
um  tu
mu  ut
fale    munaut    syk
fail    monotony  sikh
ton
tongue
flail    man tongue
Manatou
anatou
frail    anatole  sick
man toll
mental
tall
men
tell
men
Telemann
sail                kick
elephant
bail                flick
medicant
ahmed canter
amen cantor
all men can't or
tall men can
tell men
Telemann tlick
wail    element  trick
wall all it meant tick
intimate
ball                pick
intimate
Bach                click
imminent
back                clack
emanate
Braque              clock
immitate
break               cake
immolate
brick               kick
integrate
crib                kite
insulate
crab                sight
irritate        wait.......

## Poem for Kenneth Patchen

```
o o o o o o oXo o o o 0 oeoeoeoeo o o o o o o L O V E   X X
o o o o o o oXo o o 0 o 0eoeoeoeo o o o o o o           X X
o o o o o o oXo o o o0o0oeoeoeoeo o o o o o o           X X
o o o o o o oXo o o o 0 oeoeoeoeo o o o o o o           X X
o o o o o o oXo o o o o oeoeoeoeo o o o o o o           X X
o o o o o o oXo o o o o oeoeoeoeo o o o o o o           X X
o o o o o o oXo o o o o oeoeoeoeo o o o o o 0           X X
o o o o o o oXo o o o o oeoeoeoeo o o o o o o           X X
0 0          x           e e e e            o           X X
0 0          x           e e e e            o           X X
0 0          x           eeeeeeee           o           X X
0 0          x            e e e e           o           X X
0 0          x            e e e e           o           X X
0 0          x x x x x x xexexexex X x x x x0x  x x x x x x
0 0          x x x x x x xexexexeX x X x x x0x  x x x x x x
0 0          x x x x x x xexexexexXxXx x x x0x  x x x x x x
0 0          x x x x x x xexexexex X x x x x0x  x x x x x x
0 0          x x x x x x xexexexex x x x x x0x  x x x x x x
0 0          x x x x x x xexexexex x x x x x0x  x x x x x x
0 0          x x x x x x xexexexex x x x x x0x  x x x x x x
0 0  E V O L x x x x x x xexexexex x x x x x0x  x x x x x x
```

## Blues

```
    l  e
    o e
  love
  o evol
love o
  evol
 e o
e  l
```

## Easter Pome

```
   pulpit     tulips
  pul  pit   tul  ips
 pu l  p it  tu l  i ps
p u l  p i tt u l  i p s
p u l  p t iu t l  i p s
p u l  t u pl i t  i p s
p u t  u l li p i  t p s
p t u  l i up l p  i t s
t u l  i p ps u l  p i t
t u l  i p sp u l  p i t
 tu l  i ps  pu l  p it
  tul  ips   pul  pit
   tulips     pulpit
```

## Early Morning: June 23

```
                 u
              u us
             unusual
            unusual
           unusual
          unusual
         unusual
        unusual
       unusual     s
        usually    sun
       usual y    sun
      usual      sun
     usual the  sun
      al  there  nodding over his book
    belly  ere
      lys
      yellow  ringring ring ring ring
     will waveringring ring ring ring
    willowavering ring      ring ring
   winlowavering  ring ring      ring
  windowavering   ring ring ring
 windowavering    ring ring ring ring
windowavering          ring ring ring
  dow  e   g    turn        ring ring
  oworld       turno   ring      ring
  worlda      turnin   ring ring
 world now   turning   ring ring ring
  old  o     urning    ring ring ring
   dancesunderning     ring ring ring
    r  sun   ning
    k sund ring          o    u der
    lunderring        lov   under
   meanderring        over under
    y  er            over under
       rolls round and round
                          der
                          er
                          round and round
                                          my window
```

## Dada Lama

*to the memory of Hugo Ball*

1

hweeeee
hweeeee
hyonnnn
hyonnnn

hweeeee
hweeeee
hyonnnn
hyonnnn

tubadididdo
tubadididdo
hyon
hyon

tubadididdo
tubadididdo
hyon
hyon

fffffffffffffffffffffftsssssssss
ffffffffffffffffffffffitsssssssss
fffffffffffffffffffffflitsssssssss

hyonnnnnn
            unh
hyonnnnnn
            unh

2

eeeeeeeeeeeeeeeeeeeeeeeeee
EEEEEEEEEEEEEEEEEEEEEEEEEE
eeeeeeeeeeeeeeeeeeeeeeeeee

EEEEEEEEEEEEEEEEEEEEEEEEEE
eeeeeeeeeeeeeeeeeeeeeeeeee
EEEEEEEEEEEEEEEEEEEEEEEEEE

eeeeeeeeeeeeeeeeeeeeeeeeee
EEEEEEEEEEEEEEEEEEEEEEEEEE
eeeeeeeeeeeeeeeeeeeeeeeeee

3

oudoo doan doanna
tinna limn limn
la leen
untloo lima
limna doo doo

dee du deena
deena dee du
deena deena
dee du deena

ah-ooo runtroo
lintle leave lipf
lat lina tanta
tlalum cheena
ran tron tra troo

deena dee du
deena deena
dee du deena
deena dee du

da dee di do du
deena
        deena

4

AAAAAAAAAAAAAAAAAAAAA
aaaaaaaaaaaaaaaaaaaaa
AAAAAAAAAAAAAAAAAAAAA

aaaaaaaaaaaaaaaaaaaaa
AAAAAAAAAAAAAAAAAAAAA
aaaaaaaaaaaaaaaaaaaaa

AAAAAAAAAAAAAAAAAAAAA
aaaaaaaaaaaaaaaaaaaaa
AAAAAAAAAAAAAAAAAAAAA

5

tlic
tloc

tlic tloc
tlic tloc

tlic tloc tlic
tloc tlic tloc

tlic tloc tlic tloc
tlic tloc tlic tloc

tlic tloc tlic tloc tlic
tloc tlic tloc tlic tloc

tlic tloc tlic tloc tlic tloc
tlic tloc tlic tloc tlic tloc

tlic tloc tlic tloc tlic
tloc tlic tloc tlic tloc

tlic tloc tlic tloc
tlic tloc tlic tloc

tlic tloc tlic
tloc tlic tloc

tlic tloc
tlic tloc

tlic
tloc

6

wwwwwwwwwwwwwwwwwwwwwwwwwww
mmmmmmmmmmmmmmmmmmmmmmmmmmm
wwwwwwwwwwwwwwwwwwwwwwwwwww
mmmmmmmmmmmmmmmmmmmmmmmmmmm

Wwwwwwwwwwwwwwwwwwwwwwwwwww
Mmmmmmmmmmmmmmmmmmmmmmmmmmm
Wwwwwwwwwwwwwwwwwwwwwwwwwww
Mmmmmmmmmmmmmmmmmmmmmmmmmmm

WWWWWWWWWWWWWWWWWWWWWWWWWWWWWWWWW
MMMMMMMMMMMMMMMMMMMMMMMMMMM
WWWWWWWWWWWWWWWWWWWWWWWWWWWWWWWWW

0UOOOOOOOOOOOOOOOOOOOOOOOOH
MMMMMMMMMMMMMMMMMMMMMMMMMMM
0UOOOOOOOOOOOOOOOOOOOOOOOOH
MMMMMMMMMMMMMMMMMMMMMMMMMMM

FREEEEEEEEEEEEEEEEEEEEEEEEE
EEEAAAAAAAAAAAAAAAAAAAAAAAAAH
FREEEEEEEEEEEEEEEEEEEEEEEEE
EEEAAAAAAAAAAAAAAAAAAAAAAAAAH

FREEEEEEEEEEEEEEEEEEEEEEEEE
DUMMMMMMMMMMMMMMMMMMMMMMMMMM
FREEEEEEEEEEEEEEEEEEEEEEEEE
DUMMMMMMMMMMMMMMMMMMMMMMMMMM

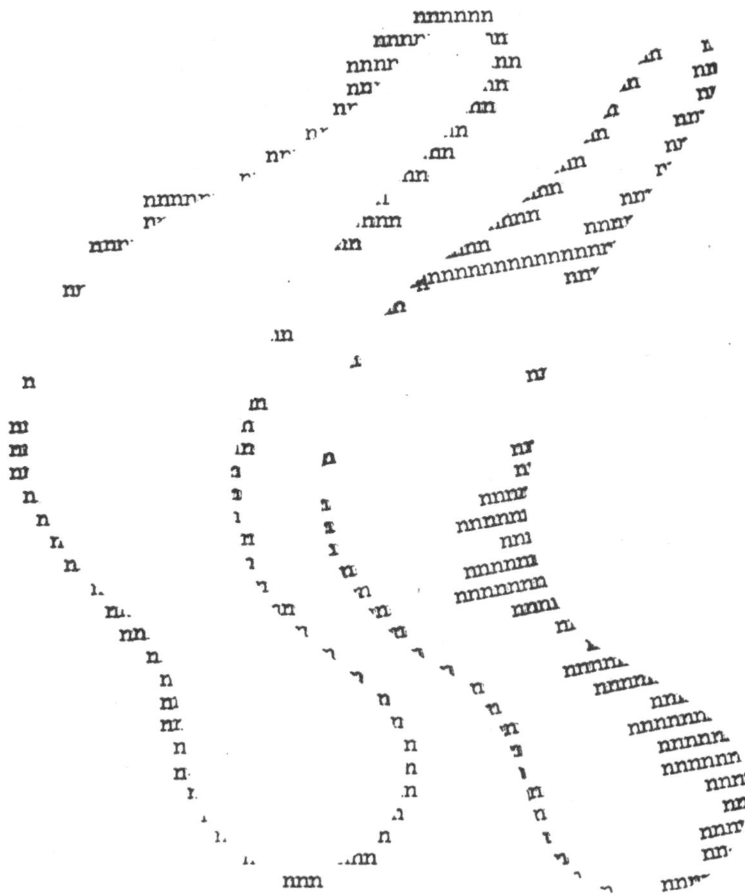

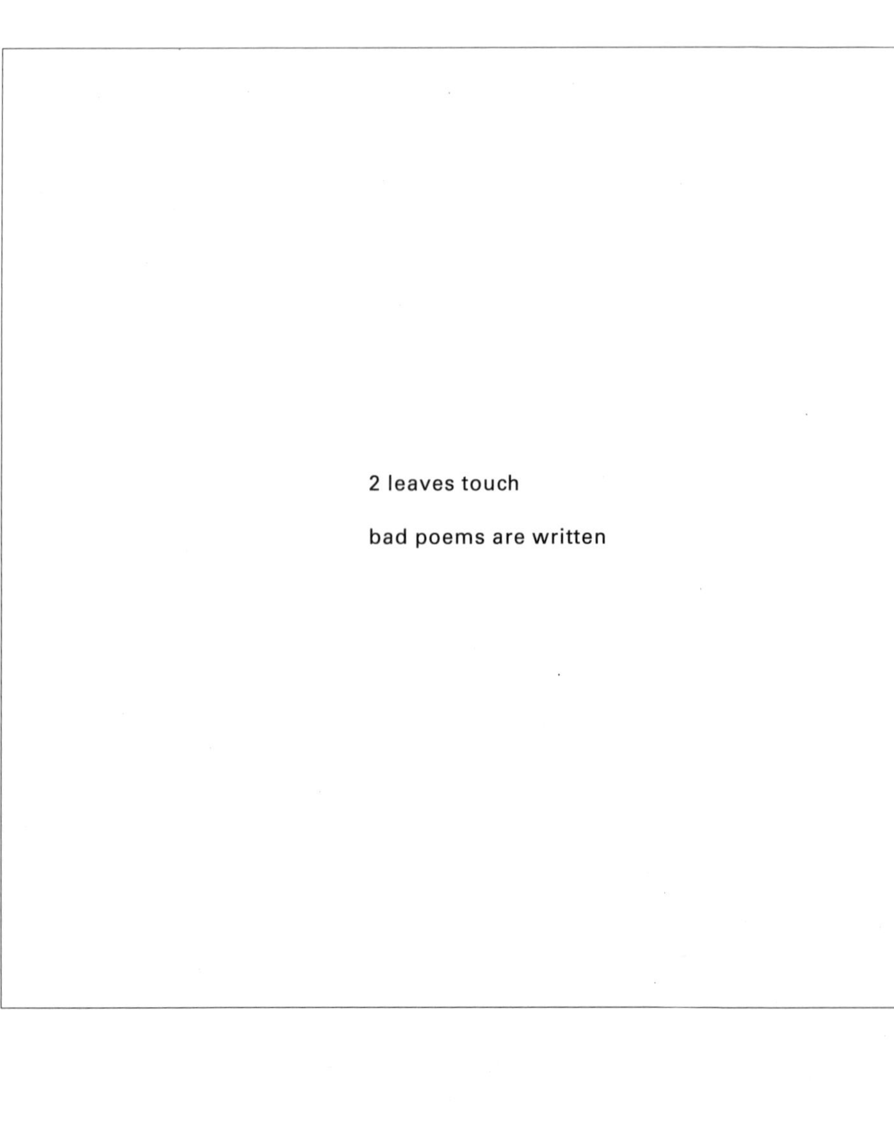

2 leaves touch

bad poems are written

st*r

moon

owl

tree tree tree shadowy

em ty

```
         )
c l ( (     ) ) d s
      (     )
         )
```

groww

blob
plop

closedpen

o      pen

## ABC: the aleph beth book

POETRY BEING AT A DEAD END POETRY IS
DEAD. HAVING ACCEPTED THIS FACT WE ARE
FREE TO LIVE THE POEM. HAVING FREED
THE POEM FROM THE NECESSITY TO BE THE
POEM IS NOW CONSTANTLY HAPPENING IN
OUR LIVES. WHAT HAS BEEN CONSTANT TILL
NOW HAVE BEEN THE ARTIFICIAL BOUNDARIES
WE HAVE PLACED ON THE POEM. WE HAVE
PLACED THE POEM BEYOND OURSELVES BY
PUTTING ARTIFICIAL BOUNDARIES BETWEEN
OURSELVES & THE POEM. WE MUST PUT THE
POEM IN OUR LIVES BY FREEING IT FROM
THE NECESSITY TO BE. WE MUST BE TO FREE
OURSELVES FROM THE NECESSITY OF PLACING
BOUNDARIES BETWEEN OURSELVES & THE POEM.
THE POEM WILL LIVE AGAIN WHEN WE ACCEPT
FINALLY THE FACT OF THE POEM'S DEATH.

ETRY BEING AT A DEAD END POETRY

HAVING · ACCEPTED THIS FACT WE ARE

REE TO LIVE THE POEM. HAVING FRE

THE NECESSITY TO BE THE

I N   O U R   L I V E S .

NOW HAVE BEEN THE

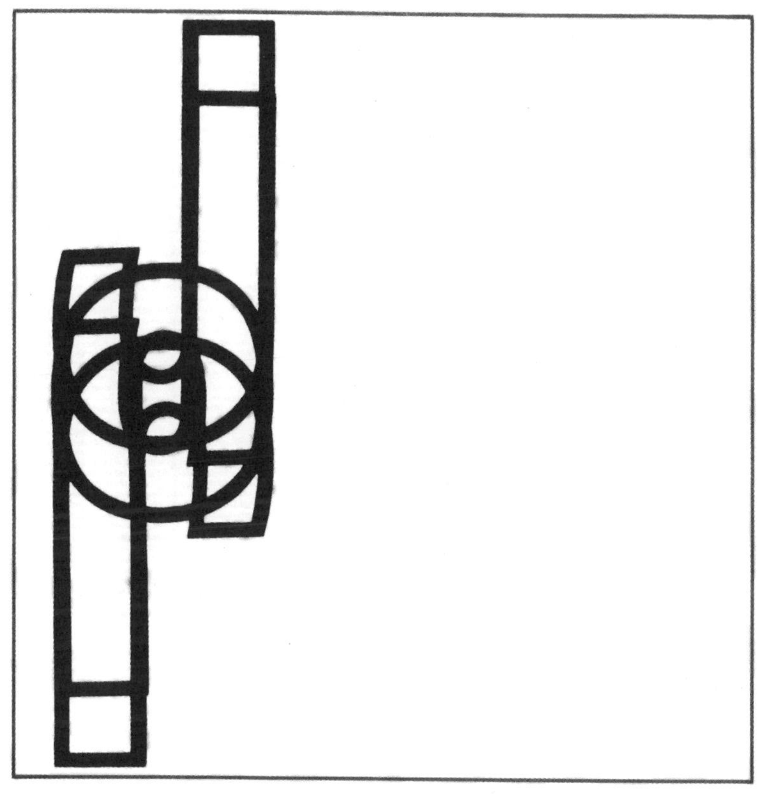

## Aleph Unit Closed

## Aleph Unit Opened

## Aleph Unit Surface

## Aleph Unit Observed

## Aleph Unit Not

## Afterword

ALEPH UNIT is a serial poem    following the principles
i had first applied in the ALLEGORIES of eliminating the
frame as a compositional unit and thereby compressing what
i had spread over a number of frames into one visual unit
(thus eliminating linear narrative and moving closer to what
i had termed in ANDY spheroid thot) i moved here to make
the Aleph shape itself the frame allowing the successive shifts
to be dominated by the memory of that *frame* of reference
(ghost image on the retina)                the movement was *in*
as opposed to horizontal or vertical moving towards not a
conclusion but a piece in which the serial process itself
articulated the unarticulated content of the specific sign the
titles suggesting what had informed each shift

*bpNichol 6 June 73*

**H (an alphhabet)**

# from The Martyrology

from *The Chronicle of Knarn*

i've looked across the stars to find your eyes

they aren't there

where do you hide when the sun goes nova?

i think it's over

somewhere a poem dies

inside i hide my fears like bits of broken china
mother brought from earth
millenniums ago

i don't know where the rim ends
to look over
into the great rift

i only know i drift without you
into a blue that is not there

tangled in the memory of your hair

the city gleams in afternoon suns.    the aluminum walls
of the stellar bank catch
                                                  the strange distorted faces of
the inter-galactic crowds.

                                                  i'm holding my hat in my hand
standing awkwardly at the entrance to their shrine
wishing i were near you.
                                                  were they like us? i don't know.
how did they die & how did the legend grow?

(a long time ago i thot i knew how this poem would go, how the
figures of the saints would emerge. now it's covered over by
my urge to write you what lines i can. the sun is dying. i've
heard them say it will go nova before the year's end. i wanted
to send you this letter (this poem) but now it's too late to
say anything, too early to have anything to send.)

i wish i could scream your name & you could hear me
out there somewhere where our lives are

we have moved beyond belief
into a moon that is no longer there

i used to love you (i think)
used to believe in the things i do
now all is useless repetition
my arms ache from not holding you

the winds blow unfeelingly across your face
& the space between us
is as long as my arm is not

the language i write is no longer spoken

my hands turn the words
clumsily

[...]

drift then as dreams
my life is lived
moment to moment the changes flow around me
it goes on too long

breaking down the ideas do
hold up the image you have made me closer to with tenderness
someone else's prayer to speak from
dave & denny's party barb came to

i remember now that i remember nothing
driving home late last night
step up to you lord
i have opened my heart for the first time
surely feelings follow

words fall
i cannot pick them up
you bend to kiss me
turn away

dave's face thru all that rain
the pain i could not tell him
it seems so jumbled
what i had thot simple to say
at best but half recalled

bright day

walk up into the clouds you seem so lost saint and
these quests take you thru the sky
follow saint rike you don't know where
step off into a deeper blue
whisper in my ear do tell me
falling with you

home

as there are words i haven't written
things i haven't seen
so this poem continues
a kind of despair takes over
the poem is written in spite of

all the words i once believed were saints
language the holy place of consecration
gradually took flesh
becoming real

scraptures behind me
i am written free
so many people saying to me they do not understand
the poem they can't get into
i misplace it three times

this is not a spell
it is an act of desperation
the poem dictated to me by another will
a kind of being writing is
opposite myself i recognize these hands
smash the keys in
the necessary assertion of reality

ah reason there is only feeling
knowing the words are
                                        i am
this moment is
everything present & tense
i write despite my own misgivings
say things as they do occur
the mind moves truly
is it free

nothing's free of presence
others pressing in
your friends assert themselves as loving you are tortured with
gradually you learn to enjoy

thus you write a history
use words you've used before
your own voice speaking in the morning whispering
holy god i do love you then praise you
take up this gift of joy
not to judge or be judged by
you who have given me lips    a tongue
the song sings because of you
all theory denies you
that struggle's truly won
once what's begun is done

[...]

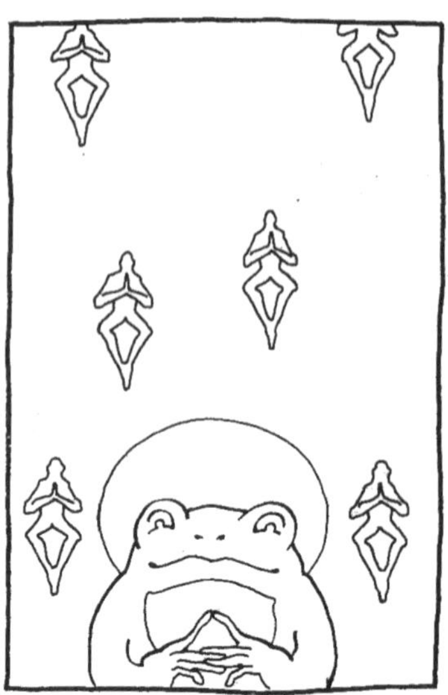

i wanted an image or a metaphor
something to contain me
within the flow of language presses in
screamed so loud my father ran to save me
not knowing i needed to fall in
that place where all space holds you

david said of the bottle in his hand
'pouring the liquid you pour the container too     gone
your skin flows out of you'
someone laughed     we were all too drunk

it is disconnected

the drinks     the ryme
the too many times not thinking for myself

the flower or the root
plucked from the ocean's floor
eaten by the snake or turtle

who knows his face        who knows
what eats what        sloughs his skin or shell &
walks away

suppose i had never come here

suppose i had done it that day
jumped from the old stone tower on big win island
pierced my body with ten stakes

i could walk the water
far as the saints would carry me
leave that skin behind & pass away

it is the full moon in the sky
the rising sun

watching from the train window
i am moved beyond it in a dream
walk the fields dumb and trembling
as in a poem i cannot remember writing
someone walks beside me whispering

thieves        THIEVES

you take a man's words to use against him
twist language to such brutal ends
i'm sick with your scheming
too lost in words to ever leave them
too full with love of speech as feeling

[...]

'you must lay down a new language, a new tongue enlightened by the spirits'
– anthony ellis

ellie & me
another form of we

rob & i or
connections
                4 or more
friends
        no ends or means
                        living

move across the prairies
planes
        geometry of abstract confession

i am nameless father
we are free to move as we please
in a land where boundaries are a frame of mind

reference

single word

visvaldis told me
'you do not take yourself seriously'
hackneyed image
                clown

you can see the way it moves now
shorter lines evolving into longer statements of place or time
the history of the poem recapitulated
last night listening to victor read
he was *there*        seated in his garden
watching the gardiner
                                        expressway?

There is no single path or token
rob & me
we drove out along that highway
west into the mid-day sun
neither of us talking
too tired from too little sleep
relaxing in the place we keeps alive for us
i thot of victor's line
remembering how i first met him        letters
i kept sending him poems        he kept rejecting them
helped dave aylward & i set up that GANGLIA reading he & margaret read at
that night the east coast of america blacked out
short circuit
                        omen
'someone up there's trying to tell us something'
dj was there
& joe
            chewing that cigar i've never known him to smoke

i call these poets friends
tho i cannot attend to them daily
there is a we
                        different        the same
links us in the law language comprehends
i have to trust to carry me thru into somewhere

driving east again
metropolitan toronto population 1,916,000
suddenly hit me
                        watching the concrete walls of the QEW
some sense of history
                            a we that lacks connections

passing the elevators
the terminal buildings
where i worked that one day burning books
the workmen in the furnace room grabbing the 1908 encyclopedias
'i want these for my kids'
i threw the rest in the incinerator
final DADA act
convinced as i was then        the uselessness of words        of print
the job made its own sense

there is no we encompasses city
only the collective place poverty or pressure brings you to
my people who are not my people
i fear you think me strange
you lacks meaning for me
becoming them

once

once when it all makes sense
the cycle which is history
                                        the sphere
gathers us in
                    we with we
a kind of litany
i know i need to bring together
my friends & my friends
make them understand each other
at least that's clear

i am afraid of writing something which does not end
as we does not
                    only the link which is i
to be replaced
                    other i's to see thru
'in the true time & space called meaning'
love as many as i can in whatever way
is that not true father?

afraid of the words even now threaten to overwhelm me i am carried away
thru the slick glass buildings        the dirty streets
the we which is not we but slabs of meat
stacked up to feed the mouths of commerce
the smoking chimneys
the burning pages of the burning books

[...]

hot night

sleepless in bed
i dreamt of nothing
tossed restlessly
talked with el

rain in the morning
air still heavy
the city is everywhere drawing nearer
i want a different music
complex but clear
carry these words to you

driving into the country
400 north towards Barrie
blue clouds in a blue sky
heavenly city
ghosts or hosts
their forms are all around us
green men in the summer woods
took the cut-off
aurora road to schomberg
'the sky is falling'
racial memory in a simpler form
the point being there are things in the sky that do fall
as that old egyptian pointed out to solon
'ah you greeks are all children'
we know so little of what could be known

speech is the holy act
linking as it does the whole body

why did i say that?

'geography is space'
west coast is sea & mountain
prairie       sky
blue here east
hills & fences
some sense of history in the 'new world'
1850 william walker exploring death valley
discovered a ruined city one mile long
its centre a huge rock almost thirty feet high
the remains of a large building on it
melted and vitrified
the indians had no tradition for it
looked on it with awe
                                        suggesting it was there before them?
Tepe Yahyā
                  there was a man
hitched into the middle east
rode the camel trains thru that timeless space
Susa       Kerman       Mohenjo-Daro
'the name of the present world is place'
crossed from the Tigris to the Indus basin
back again towards Bahrein
the greek 'springs of Ocean'
Dilmun

oh father
blinded as he was by grief gilgamesh found death for his trouble
& the hitch-hiker watched it all
seated behind the speaker as he always is
i wish he'd speak to me sometime

there is a city grows around us in these woods
a history which is american vespuchi never knew
Tiahuanco
                gate of the sun
oldest city on earth
one theory has it culture spread from there
over Atlantis Mu
Oz (as cayce mentioned)
into Egypt & the east
huge blocks of stone fitted within 1/100th of an inch
technology we still lack the tools for

the city outlives us all          the we
we talk as if it were the enemy
as we use the word american derogatorily
meaning 'that bastard from the united states'
we lack any sense of real community
define ourselves in terms of what we don't want to be
give the symptoms the control
talk about our helplessness
as saint and did
played that game of distances
never wanting to get close

walking towards the woods
saw the groundhog disappearing in the grass
running from me
who brings the smell of city with him
that kind of death it's come to mean
carried along
                    one bird          another
song          deeper into wood
dark places where the light is hooded by the leaves
stand silent          tip the head back          blue
imagine a point where the waters meet
ocean to river to lake to stream
overland to here

i thot i heard your sails creak SAINT ORM

i thot the clouds were you

[...]

there is a sign comes

'it rained' julia said
i hadn't thot of it that way

it's true

that spring we returned to
thru the back roads beyond mono centre
the signs said PRIVATE PROPERTY

listening to the rain
remember a time on comox
andy dave barb & me
                                        that form of we
place        vancouver
time         1963
leave here now
bare feet in the wet earth
rows of carrots & peas
new foal in the pasture
born this morning
                                        5 a.m.

always there is something younger & helpless needing you
is that the other sign father
that there are things we must do to help we
fulfill our destiny wherever it leads us
standing in the rain in dufferin county
walk over to the town line
mono & adjala townships
                                                            there is no way to encompass everything
we need to encompass as much as we can

the pain is the recognition the work outlives us
we die before we's completion
                                                                     whatever that is
these memories of vancouver       an older time
are memories of a we that never worked
existed in a timelessness which is not memory
only a standing still as years go past
a lack of destiny

earlier today
woke from sleep
a frog in my room
caught it
carried it outside
                                              it pissed in my hand
terror of me
let it free in the rain & mud
watched it hop away
thru the orchard the field
where my eyes go most every day
a sense of possibility
watch the clouds pile up days the sun shines
thinking of that place the saints left behind
dissolving community
the fall from place into space
an earth they never felt at home on

it is a question of heritage
reclaiming the myths that give us history
a geography of time

a chance you have given me father
for which i thank you

[...]

now that it's over
now that the long road's gone
your wife dead your tongue stilled saint orm
we are left as we are always left
moving on

after the thinking thru
after the theories run their course
after the instances of forced conclusions
realities thrust upon you you cannot escape
the knowledge that life is that tension between
the public & the private
the we & the i remain
the lack of conclusions is the same
the superior man moves as he stands in the flow of it
learns to sing
                              happy to be more than that single thing
those others around him he attempts to know
endless learning which is living

6:05 a.m.

halifax december morning

roy in the other room writing
me in the kitchen getting this down

now i am here
4 hours puts the here there
mind already travelling ahead
down the dark streets
under the trees towards the harbour
waiting for the bus to pick me up
begin the journey back towards toronto

everything comes together

the sound of roy's typewriter
the image of your face
this sense of place which is canada
everything strung out in a line
narrative runs thru
all life a sphere we move within
poets friends lovers saints
caught up in
carried out on
the current of a we which is history
language our currency
banked in time
laying down the base for what's to come

6:30

blue light against the buildings
edges of the blue sails
move out in early morning
over the ocean
where they came from

we

[...]

from the lake's edge        ontario
the city rises        the hill
just north of admiral road
you climb        taking the highway        up
the roads take you
out of toronto over the flat stretches        hills
reaching the top of the old lake bottom
dufferin county
                    cloud range stretched above you
i so wanted to walk
long as the mind remembers that vision

standing here        history is the sea that covered you
the great lakes are memory & what you can't remember
where the larvae mutate (one reported last year
18 times its normal size)
                    utnapishtim or noah
they are both the same saint orm
built boats
set forth when the flood came
sailed above me
closer to the cloud range
where you slept in your ignorance of what went below
passed on that dark sea
unaware of each other
set down on mountains at the flood's end
it is a tale we all know

[...] that one went down into hell (the earth)
& up into heaven (the sky)
the question of why such connections is never answered

that one goes west (to vancouver)
or east (to halifax)
is a matter of facts        geography
placing yourself relative to 4500 miles of country
whatever the journeys up or down that might have gone
have yet to come before you

[...]

last take

late february 73

dave & i look out towards the lion's gate

years mass<br>
        events<br>
we made it out between the lion's paws<br>
rear shocks gone<br>
swerving to avoid the bumps<br>
spell of spelling cast around us<br>
tiny ripples in the blood stream the brain stem's rooted in<br>
a body place &<br>
        time<br>
the lion's month before us the lamb's born in<br>
the door<br>
     you are not permitted to open again<br>
enter thru the lion's mouth the man's root gets planted in<br>
*not* to be consumed<br>
             as tho the use of lips weren't speech<br>
a doorway into the woman's soul intelligence comes out of<br>
SCREAMING<br>
         a complete thot<br>
born from the dialogue between you

or what comes forth from my mouth
born from the woman in me
handed down thru my grandma ma & lea
is what marks me most a man
that i am finally this we
this one & simple thing
my father Leo
my mother Cancer
                                        she births herself
the twin mouths of women
                                              w's omen
it turns over & reverses itself
the mirrors cannot trick us
our words are spun within the signs our father left
the sibilance of s
                                     the cross of t
there are finally no words for you father
too many letters multiply the signs
you are the one
                              the unifying
no signifier when we cannot grasp the signified
saints in between
                                      the world of men
women
                          the sign complete
the w & the circle        turning
add the E
                           the three levels
linked by line
                                 or the two fold vision
H to I
                  the saints returned to this plane

the emblems were there when i began
seven years to understand
the first letter/level of
                                             martyrdom

*CODA: Mid-Initial Sequence*

faint edge of sleep
a literal fuzzing in the mind
as tho the edge of
what was held clearly
became less defined
the penalty paid &
your father recognized
for what he is

for W

HA!

the is

[...]

the wind outside rises

air
    grey
day
    janvier
moment when the movement changes
the line straightens out & stretches on ahead
there's room to pass
out into the flats of heaven
the cloud land
a night's sleep has seen the last of
for the moment
momentum carries us
on in our arc around the sun
& the lines become as long as the tongue can
                    / carry without breathing in

images shift
                    blue sky turning back to grey

it is the wind moves it

it is a language the celts knew & spoke of

runes
    (the running e's)
pass as vowels thru energy

consonants as nouns

vowels as verbs

what are the sentences that form
words they're made of
syntax of alignment i want to see
apparent in every bush & tree
placement of the sea & land
a plan
        not in the sense of plot
pre-conceived
but there
            readable
if i am able to
see man
             writable
purpose
            breaks skin's surface
gains control
moves from the know        on
into the un
prefix delimiting the road
out of the two year darkness of the mind
no music i could find to lead me
sick of ending things before their time
is marked

             b
eaten up
's sung in
             the bottom range
down the upper
twists of phrase

sur visage
the mouth opens
writing following the o of
sound
        noise
products of the human voice

awaking
too little sleep
now falls
                    beyond the wind
o
   w forms
at the word's end
word's beginning is
the book's end
that conundrum
vision
riddle we are all well rid of
the dull pass of wisdom

w is d
o ma
i 'n h and
the me's restated
at the pen's tip's ink
at the tongue's noise
w in d
              din
Blake's vision of
Golgonooza

after noon
the clouds give way to sky
blue
         e
le me 'n
t
  always
why

to rid me of
the ugh in
thought
i spell anew
weave the world
out of the or
binary
          the note spun
out of the dinary into the few
letters i am granted
signs
        to reach who i cannot touch
miles & years between us

february 1 1975 5:48 p.m.
conscious i may be dead when you read this
as two nights ago i lay awake
trying to grasp the concept 'infinite'
a feeling of vertigo
i am so much less than everything
the fact of the all
encompassing me

                            gunning into high
digger digger
the cat gut &
the fiddler
                questions to answer
answer's an A
                    B
ginning
            of the town
the saints came down from
buildings crumbling
middle ground abandoned
the road takes me
into the centre of that emptiness
the past is made by
the present

at root the blue is bleu
means ‘bright’
if you get the b right
everything’s ginning
essents & essentials
so much of the problem is misnaming

last night
              walking home
stars above the church at the foot of Huron
the sky a darker blue to purple
range i cannot name
that activity
what should be play
too often’s re-creation
the change that Langtek worked
‘wreck-creation’
foreign to me now
                              i want the world
absolute & present
all its elements
el
  em
      en
          t’s
o
  p q
      r

or b d
                bidet
confusion of childhood’s ‘kaka’
the Egyptian ‘KA’
                                  soul
rising out of
the body of
the language

the streets are not named
standing in the centre square
staring up at windows they no longer gaze from
the whole point of it ended
meanings for existence
gone
the stuttered b
ing
that is living
stammer thru our days
impotent in less obvious ways than
the limp dick or
frozen ocean of
response
the saints come down to
their mortality
or fled
to live among the dead
outside our memories
the city that they built
a memo re
a son
one's debt to one's father
forgotten
farther away than
the next star or
page
surface that the eye lights on

in the press of speech
awkward words are chosen
that decision is
the voice's prelude
skeletal remains
apparent in
the choice of
building blocks

the 'b' locks into place

a command

in the space left
the weight of air shifts
visible compounds of earth & water
within a balanced sphere of
forces

fire (which is sun)

air

earth & water (clouds)

air

earth & water (earth)

fire (which is core & molten)

we can journey outward
into hell
the suns & darknesses of space
or inwards
into cave-black liquid stone &
fire
at the earth's core
old questions i had asked
answered
Lucifer fell
from fire onto earth & could not rise again
burrowed into
the ground

the meteor in northern siberia
June 30th 1908
'a sound was heard
louder than ... thunder
and a column of fire
... shot skyward'

'a farmer living fifty miles away
was hit by a heat wave
which he feared would set fire to his clothing'

i burn on the inside
unnamed purpose
as i had dreamed it years ago
to write my way thru the books of the dead
let the process take me
thru
into
the books of the living

& i move now
out of 3
          into 4
or 1
     some new beginning
sensed here
amid the sensory sensation of
speech
          these words
the arch
ark
    Io
logical
          invocation of
the change
               flames i saw
among the monotones
the burning beasts
                         cattle
Io of the many eyes
Nura Nal's vision Io who suckled Zeus
& 'invented the five vowels of
the first alphabet
                         & the consonants
B & T'
               Nura Nal who sees thru dreams
what is to transpire
that arch which takes us
over the present
                         into the future
arks we sail
like Noah or Utnapishtim
till we come to that day
we are no longer young
others come
               as Gilgamesh did
caught up in
the immortality game
to question us

there is no one here to question

the wind howls in the empty streets
shutters bang uselessly
i pick my way thru the remnants of their speech
the crumbling outline of their modes of thot
i am no closer to them
only further away from earth
dizzy from the lack of air
i stumble frequently

in the long hours the heart is slowed
the mind drifts between the particles
letters of the law
the B is born
                                        one day before
the celebration of your son Lord
according to the Bethluisnion
& i sit
late in the Nth month
waiting for the F to dawn
seven days from now
ash dropping from
the fire i have lit in my hand

the B gins us
A's the birth
tree
day of
                    celebration
I
  the death
yew
loss of we
which is our perfect B
ginning
                      false pride of individuality
that i am
                                      yes
but i was of
came from
                                    this soil
W
     o men
we all begin in
that embrace our M's contained in

here
'where the sea sleeps'
'where the cold is unendurable'
in these 'barbarous lands at
the end of the world'
we are caught in
a tangled dreaming
an immigrant nation of
uncertain history
we are like you saints
the lands we left destroyed
by nothing more than
the hours' passing

tonight
the moon shines
thru this house of glass
as i as well had said it
'the poem is dead
                                        long live the poem'
i know now the saints were wrong
demigods at best
we have struggled a millennium
without your name
no power to invoke but our own
noun of your being absent
no other nouns cohere

i speak from 'the land of the summer stars'
'at the back of the north wind'
where the souls flock
each spring
the ponds & hills of
dufferin county
set out food at the pond's edge
because it is right & necessary
wander the woods where the old beeches stand
books of your being
light green of new leaves
blue spring sky
that colour range which is the saxon word 'glas'
& it is death i see
which is the absence of the strength to call you
the power to invoke your name
gone in the shifting game of allegiance
your jealous children played
& i am left wanting you
left to amuse myself
mother/father
i am afraid
retreat to theory
talk factually when i feel unsure
hate the noise of such didacticism
hate my hatred of it

journal journey
jour de nalney
move slowly thru the signs of passage

[...]

'you are dead saints'
given back into the drift of print
of speech
                    born anew among the letters
a different tension
                                    different reach
of logic
            of the mind's playing out of
reason
                a rhyme
till God's re sonned
on the tongue
the groan that must accompany your birth lord
l or d
                unless the el's read 'one'
one ord er
absolute & true
which is the two tone order of the pun

[...]

a road
a rod

a walk along

a long day
a dying night

an art
a log

a journal that is right
here
        ere i begin[2]
among the streets & houses stand around me
How Land over the bridge
(du pont) to Daven's Port
& in between a sea (mer)
Wal
        full tragedies are played
accomedies
                        points of view:      St George & St Clair
never meet
                        (he goes to College & becomes Beverley)
fits together in its own sense
St George to separate
Admiral & Huron     history
i should've traced
                              race
against race
against
                      time
rimes of
coincidence
                        (sense arrived at in
a later reading
latter writing
related rewrite of

tone

note

placement of
St Ick or Ylus in
the hierarchy

St Iff if if fits

(alternate spellings
suggested by
George Pal in
Dr Omic's St Andard Dictionary))

---

SWITCH

---

i live on Brun's wick
so named 'cause it stuck out
thick as his legendary stick
into that wal of water flowed
around the foot of Casa Loma
licked its way between
the hill that castle stands on &
Russell's Hill
                                        or south
stretching round the ruins of what was
Harbored
                        Harbour D
(a harmony)
only puns someone says
i says glimpses of another truth
'nother story worth the tell
'll do as well as Mag Mell
Olympus or
Shanghalla
all the old bars the saints'd gather at
this new one come into our ken

understand (?)

i 'understand' all i didn't see before
connect these fact zones
create fictions
as someone (Brun?) did before me
if i read the map aright
'Brun's wick ken'd al[l]'[3]

set ablaze by light
it was the light!
a candle
            (Kendal)
burning

hierarchies suggested in a reading

Wal Mer's pa Dina Madi'[s] son
(her one &
only)   images of
ancient lineages

St Orm the saint of ships & seas
was he Wal Mer's father
Dina Madi's son
& if the one
then all these names could be
nicknames
for claimd similur things

(Wal Mer stretches south
into the bluer strait
streets
          houses lived in in my time
short tho it's been
one-third gone
still learning
trying to move on)

more than the grand gestures aspired to
actions give the truth of speech
content of a daily life
                              our struggle
(ideals arrayed against the actual i deals) each morning
step out that door
onto this wick forms part of the shore
head north for the bridge
rise early
get to work before the sky turns grey with smoke
worlds of dreams & felt feelings
memories evoked of childhood despair
lost loves & lustres in this present world they are too present in
struggle to return them to the past again
archaeo logically

walked today        west thru snow        across Dupont
frozen streets/seas        thot then of Kit James
dead this past year
caught myself (briefly) wondering
'what's Kit doing?'
but he is done
one takes so long accepting
the death of friends/
                                /relationships
new twists your life takes
'in the inner circle of communication
the poet is opposed on two sides of thought'
& i am mourning his passing
                                                caught up in the snow
Spadina
        a dirt road
trucks rumbling north for the subway's construction
underground
                underworld
under wal
        mermur
murmer
        mer made memories
white world of whispered presences
(Kit?)

death's   deed's   done
dēath's   dead's   dōne
d'ath's   d'ad's   d'n

& gone

        'gin ag'in th'n

on

   as snow's gone
spring's come
changes tone's tune
my foots moved            on
the poem accumulates its clarity
its imprecisions

decision:
lift my foot
in march
out the snow
fresh fallen
set it down in april
when the flow
resumes

it is
enough

i would be
done
with all this
dying

would wake my friends
from
their dreadful sleeps of
false
reason

reason enough to mourn

reason enough to rail against a world

no use getting hung up on a word

no use not speaking

say it

& then

(moving this very spring
north to Warren Road
above Russell's Hill & Poplar Plains
above the port that Daven named
the ford where St George laid his bed
hoping to woo St Clair there
she lies north of me instead
impervious to his need

between Poplar Plains & Russell's Hill
some evidence of war &
whatever battle fought there
ends where these two come together
north of the port the bridge now crosses[4]
as this bridge must
connect two states of consciousness
written weeks apart
form a link your mind can follow
paths my thots had taken
transparent connections
'and' composed of forty-two words
makes it possible to travel from
'the bridge now crosses' to
'walk thru the park past the castle on my way to work'
deleting quotes (take up this speech again)

southern fringe of Forest Hill
ravines & bridges
                    (under & over)
another bridge
                    pont
pointed along it as i walk
angered by this morning's meeting
not really part of this poem
part of my life only
only part of the life this poem grows from
my own)

early july day
heading north from Toronto
Ebenezer      Wildfield
crops already taken off the land & bundled
sheep grazed gullies
summer sequences
first herds long gone from these barns
outside the city
                    numbers replace the names
subdivisions of a larger purpose
a reading changes
left at Chinguacousy Township 31st sideroad
right at Sandhill
                    north east on the 6th line
                                        Peel Regional Road 7
                                        Airport Road

3 names for just this one path chosen
sped thru Mono Road
past the left turn to Inglewood
down the hill & into Caledon East
paused to take note of the poem

when you travel on the naming changes
Caledon left        Albion right
i drive the border line
signs warn of deer
over the hills
                                        Mono Mills
pause again the road's renamed
Dufferin County 18
                                                            take note
as i have before
                                            invoked its sign if only partially
i seek to inscribe the net of names & numbers encloses me

401 west to Kitchener
pass thru escarpment south of Halton Hills
cliffs to the left
edges of
perception        re
new ways of
sea
            ing's
                                        old line's
ghost geography
sail the lost lake bottom
Ellie & me        a thousand other cars
cross the crossed out
ross the rossed out
sea cedilla
softened slipping under
disappears in eternity

we will not drown in this july air
tho one hurls one's lines
as a drowning man
or a falling fool
might
                                    praying for
connection
some bridge between himself & the void that threatens

drivin' long
writin' poems that come out song
sound tracking a life

Galt Preston Hespeler
they are all gone
one sign now
so many forms set my teeth to clicking
semblances of speech
                                        change
even as you pass them

driving Huron County
pass thru Shakespeare      Stratford &
the river Avon
language & its shapers
colonization of the Huron tongue
i find i cannot stop these readings

'he reads too much into it'
'he read the signs aright'
'i stayed up half the night'
                                                    'doing what?'
'reading ...'

when Victor's mother died
he sent out the card that read AWAKE

these words are simply signs
signs i read as other words
messages i saw that time
wrote the phrase
'clues to unlock the secret mind'
thinking i hid the key
the tumbler's clicking awakened me

up before dawn's missed
tracing cardinal signs
North Easthope left
South Easthope right
we are driving into that east our hope resides in
what maps yield

dictating lines as they occur
revising when the moment comes
on      headlights
blurred by fog      ellie's hand
shapes the letters so unlike my own
infinite variety of form & pressure
indexed by the measure chosen

Nith River
New Hamburg to the left
Wilmot Township
sky lightening in the east
the most & least that could be written of
put an order to the mind's perceptions
make them mine
d to e
            shift
work with those occurences extend
dependent on that play to say the line ends or
continues

second take      september 3 76
Forest Road passed beyond
the boundary of a city
sequences fall      Stratford
Shakespeare
                    New Hamburg next
'Little Europe'
                    South Ontario
the counties go      Perth/Waterloo/Huron/& on
it's Toronto i return to
'r onto toro 'n to T.O.
ronto Lord
let my praise or love of thee
substain me when death comes
tho there be no greater plan beyond our lifespan
no plan even then
let that be enough

(ending on a definite note
moves the poem forward
like a foot
            a foot note

[...]

2

arch a is m

a connection seen
bridges tween
four to five
an afternoon & then an evening
                                                            nap

pan
        pun
vowelgrrgyrations pon
pinning
              down
pen
                that ponders only when
the writer's home
de
      script
                tion

door

                hall

an opening
a friend

permission

then?

                    change of tone

'i remember the first time when …'
thus it is that you begin
                                        a conversation
moves from the window to the door
over the crowded floor of
the room

                    too many rymes or
                    coincidents the placid flow of th
                    ink ing

in k

in g (in be

*tween) h i j in the tree n*

*its blue*

winter day

straight thru the passed glass

see it as it was the way the bird

sat there on the branch

a word in a poem

self-evident

i was seven years old

th

in

on

un

pretentious

conscious

force is

the im age

the hero has left the stage

replaced by the horror comic schemer

dreamed his downfall in his dark rage

filled with nothing but his own envy

his wish to be

there

in the longed for spotlight

paging differently

calling up the ones i still believe in

can still talk it whole[5]

emotion ideation a unity

there is a hole there

behind the w

the emptiness shows thru

these configurations spellings

evoke the feelings we cannot pretend are strangers

'the precision of openness'

a phrasing

phasing passed thru

nothing's final in itself
only tools you use
breaking thru
                    'the unyielding word'
into that world of feeling governs you

picture a man (31) narrating this poem

picture a man (36) typing this final draft

picture the man they speak of
who is almost them

picture the man who writes
(myself)
          a pose or the real thing?

& picture me
spoken of by the man telling
telling in my turn

they are all me
one way
          not me
another
          tightened focus rather
centre of a principle uncertainty

begin again then

                         the road

begin again

                    the log's an art

begin again
begin again
begin again
}
← that song

it is a cycle i have chanted

a season in its turn

a statement of position

given its due
there's no need to hold it up to you

he is not a hero in his various guises
he is not a saint or figure to be saved
he is himself

sometimes the things we say are one & the same

he bears my name

he cannot bear it
& he shifts
h to i &
e to f
              if
stiff saint of gratitude & heartlessness
hazard of chance
never to abolish
born from death's tumble
die & be cast
                     translated
equated from you Lord

$\frac{\text{G to h to i}}{\text{D to e to f}}$
                         line being O unbending
the eternal mystery of Your presence in the world
we come out of G(O)D into the shift of probability
possibility born

b
or n (first or last
name
                  choice is false
i claim them both)
signs      monsieur ord
sighin's ici's peech
(qu'est-ce que c'est?)
sayings worked in as a saw
seen surface surfeit

arm of God
clear light the sun
rises as in a symphony
oboes play
systematically, brilliantly, the sound
totters on the edge of language
ici le soleil
ceçi says he
seizes the line

time, t'me, tatters
shatters the shhhhh leaping
baababits of
shpeech

(name's fame's fin
ally
(alley oops)
l e
thend
&
n

am i my own last word?
conjunction tween a past world & the next?
or anti-past
a-historical
i tied to my own life of
fictions
friction rubs the daily thread of?[7] or
o
dropped from the mouth of

God
Lord
Holy
Ghost
Host?

G L H G H

7 12 8

7 8

saint

            saint

27 15 42

9

6 6

21

      3

a trinity
sliding out of
a numerology

david speaking: 'a number by itself means nothing'
i said: 'nothing by itself means nothing'
lionel was tracking the word shift: 'laughter in slaughter'
some speak of joy in all that suffering

the message was thy love wasn't it?

I do forget about that listening Lord

even in my ignorance i know
you are
            i am
                  me
              em.
                   ma
peel de light de lips spil.        sam tips.
i saw he keeps
ten or one t' tell to
of one lost sole no foot'l let ten or one t' speek .

eh?

             was i spit ma's lips spil()ed?

sam didn't catchem then –
but what's with all this dick tracing
pat pattin' of the past?
between the b & m's the dirth
& b & m's a birth dance of its own
part of the mirthology

reworking one book
or rebooking work one
or one work re book &
gee
      in the s peek
eek is
part of the equation
quation's hung from an e informs the scream
cream only if the c reams
eak my love & eek my fear
follow these vowel changes for what they teach me[7]

v v

dis pair

birds

birdens

a bunch of frozen d's

gesticulation

books 4 & 5 &

books 1 to 3

(morning) ↖
means

i am
the major question of the a.m.

9 o's &
one that seems to wrinkle seems
unformed
like a thot

a footnote or consideration

a join in the pleasure ring

12

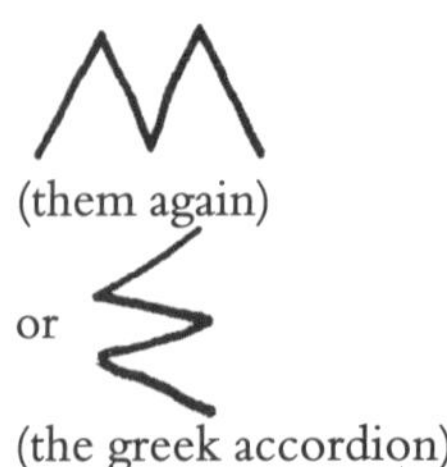

(them again)

or

(the greek accordion)

the joining of dis pair
however they care to carry themselves
as omen or
the double you
know you'll meet
walking down the street towards you
a ranger st.
moves out beyond one
into the world

you picked up this book today
read the lines i wrote
seated 'cross the table from Mary
writing in her apartment on St George
the things we talked about
(her writing
some joke or two shared
read me from the memoir she is working on)
flow on unnoticed
our bones already rotted as you read this poem
far enough beyond the present i cannot imagine you
death pokes its head into the text
stage managing as always &
departs
the heart of the process
impossible to convey tho i wish to
cups of coffee drunk &
cigars smoked
are not, finally, the book you hold

place the pen on the notebook page once more

it is all too self-conscious
like life itself

the two equated
in a single
f
  p
    t
      ex
          act
type set &
*book born*
clonely
(contradictions in a single term)
more than a pair
carries these fixed gestures towards you

i am moving before you get the chance to move
writing out the book's already written
present's past tense in the present's
work outdistancing the theory
made old as me by time
essayed a poem with all the process prose is
the play in line a thrust defines
forward back[10]

september 6th 1980

september 6th somewhere in a head ahead

(i waited these two years for these last lines to come
'carrying it all the time like a baby')

[...] **A Note On Reading *The Martyrology Book V***

Book V was structured on the idea of the chain – chain of thot, chain of images, chain of events – so that in the writing when a branching of thot occurred i would try to follow all the chains that opened up. Hence, in the text, what may appear like footnote numbers actually represent reading choices. As a reader you can continue thru the chain of ideas you're already following, or you can choose, at different points, to diverge & follow the chain of ideas the various numbered options represent (the numbers corresponding to the twelve different chains in the text). This means, of course, that no two readers will necessarily have the same experience of Book V, tho they will walk away with a similar sum. The gordian knot that Book V seems to become is also an untying of the first four books. In Book VI (which is coming into existence despite published statements to the contrary) this leads on into a number of independent, but conceptually & thematically linked, books. A book which is books & the chains of thot that thot will eventually lead into & out of.

Toronto, May 30th 1982

minus the ALL ABOARD

minus my father waving

minus the CN logo

minus my mother waving

minus seventeen years of my life
Ellie & me
our unborn child in her belly
heading east
out of Vancouver
July 27th
8 p.m.
nineteen eighty-
1.

*

what i wanted to write:
'this is how it begins' or
'pulling into New Westminster'

what actually happened:
took a different route
skipped the canneries of New Westminster entirely

(so much for nostalgia or
plotting the poem in advance)

walking up to the snack bar
seven cars to the front
the sleeping car porter three cars ahead
making the beds
the teenage kid said to him
(admiringly) 'you've got it all worked out eh'
as he flipped the mattress down
upper to lower
berth
            & the porter said
'if i had it all worked out
i wouldn't be doing this'

★

crossing the Fraser River
Port Mann in the night
lights out the left window of
the train

darker outline of the mountains
dark blue of the sky
minus the stars
out this left window on the universe

★

the old guy who spoke to the porter just now said:
'my wife wanted to take this trip
before she takes her heavenly trip'

my grandma, 96, earlier today said:
'i don't think i wanta stay around too many more'

Ellie's sitting across from me
reading Peter Dickinson's *One Foot In The Grave*
& in the first draft of this poem i wrote:
'minus these coincidences
what is the world trying to tell me?'

minus – the word returns
– some notion of absence (not a life)
subtracting the miles travelled east
(minus mine – us)
loosing all notion of possession
aboard this mixed metaphor

★

upper berth swaying in the darkness
click as the wheels clack off the miles

two women pass thru
drunk from the observation car
the one talking at the top of her voice
i say 'shut up' loudly

the woman shuts up
& her friend
lowering her voice whispers back
'fuck off'

lullabies in the real world

★

insistent instances

Kamloops in the early morning

someone, going crazy in their roomette,
rings the porter's bell repeatedly

seven a.m.

no way to sleep again

stagger forward to breakfast
the eggs taste of plastic or pam

drink tea
lurch up to the observation car
watch the mountains loom by

back in the sleeper car
one porter scratches the other porter's knees
'stop it! you know what that does to me!'

Blue River at ten
my cousin Donna's nursing station visible thru the trees

you too, Nicky,
none of us escapes these details
presences
even in these wilds
rocking back & forth
eastward on this western train

★

beginnings & endings

discrete frames in
a continuous flow

the japanese family talking
words i don't know

a horse glimpsed from the window
a man at the river's side
things i have knowledge of but cannot account for

like the flowers i saw
earlier today
purple spikes driven up
interspersed among the charred stumps of the fired forest

or the mountain's high green meadow
visible above the clouds

or the brook the train crossed even as i wrote these words
rushing down
carrying its content
into the larger lakes & rivers of the world

★

'because i was raised on trains'
– this is the line that kept recurring to me
all night

'because i criss-crossed the west with
my mother & father'
– the only line i could find to write
remembering
as the woman across from us slaps her son's fingers
spilling the peanuts my father bought
all down the aisle of the train, 1954,
or dad yelling at me, 1948,
because i was running back & forth to the water cooler,
the newsy's face that same trip,
pissed off at his job,
twisted in a grimace i was intended to read as genial

random information intrudes each time i ride these rails
maybe for the last time
headline in that Vancouver paper
GOVERNMENT AXES TRANS-CONTINENTAL LINE THRU JASPER
part of my memory disappears
1500 jobs & a slice of history

'because i criss-crossed the west with
my mother & father'

'because i was raised on trains'

*

the conductor takes our luncheon reservations
'1:15'

but at five to 1 says 'it's five to 2 –
set your watch ahead'

nothing's fixed aboard this paradox
affects more than we believe

flux logic

we eat at 2:15

*

ten minutes outside of Jasper
the line between sadism & masochism is drawn

as his one year old son hits his other son with a wire brush
the father across from us says to him:
'hit yourself with it!'

masochism wins –
the kid starts hitting himself
at least once for every time he hits his brother

WHACK WHACK

following this tack
hitting the track to town

*

'too much like a rock song'
– what i thot as i ended the previous poem

how come that voice keeps butting in?

why the need to resolve parameters?

why not the rush of
the asymetrical
arhythmic
world?

why not the y <u>not</u> the z
in the unwritten alphabet ahead?

★

okay we'll start there
with st utter's subtler statement

when the riddle's rid of rid
dle remains
ashine with its own kind of mystery

half words
half visions

the train pulls out of Jasper
three hours late

is this the st ate of my mind
or does that saint exist
beyond these twisting tracks
the train of thot?

★

so there it is

the literal metaphor or symbol

linear narrative of random sequential thots

accidents of geography, history & circumstance

the given

★

i don't like the 'symbol'
except as accent to the basic drum
of consciousness

i don't like the 'like'
except as entrance to
a "pataphysical reality

i like the play of words
of life    the moment when the feelings focus
   absolutely    a description

which is what st ate meant?    yes
the st ate meant
this

*

whistle

pulling over the level crossings
in the gathering dark into Edmonton

drainage ditches gleaming in the last light
clusters of buildings & trees

as night falls the sky reverses
dark clouds against a lighter blue

& the mind reverses
sleep takes
loosing the dream you

*

two hours from Saskatoon
fingernail of moon in the eastern sky
the pastel gray clouds at dawn
blow over the pinkening horizon
train gathering speed all the while
the berth shakes back & forth &
forth over the prairie

the revelation is in the blue dome of air
beneath which this train & the dawn appear
blue as the robin's egg i found age two
shattered on the sidewalk
bits of curved blue flung all about
& the train of thot it led to

blue as that imagined sky that day
when the clouds were white
& the prairies lay over the mountains
in my future

*

mist of rain across the far horizon

heading out of Saskatoon
6:35 a.m. July 31st
the sky is a constant gray
& the fields of wheat, alfalfa, clover, grass, etc.
stretch away for miles in all directions

encompassed we make our way
thru the middle of Canada
east towards Winnipeg

the mid-summer morning rain

these middle days

*

later
a cultivator
then an elevator

somewhere between  Nokomis & Raymore
(Semans to be exact)
two perfect stone circles
in a playground beside the tracks
except the circles are made of old tractor tires
(i can see this as we draw closer)

like that day
looking for the stones of Shap
saw a perfect circle beyond the crest of the next hill
lost sight of as we raced down into the valley, thrilled,
up & over, it was gone,
only a raggedy row of sheep in that field beyond

this is how the world is
rimes that disappear as you draw closer to their sense
dense clumps of trees
scattered across the open fields
notation
in the landscape of a nation &
a revelation

★

vanishing

down into the valley
tracking a forgotten river bottom
thru the farms, the ordered fences,
this old order is all around us
as we cross the border into Manitoba

saints you are gone
part of an older order of this poem
as Brun, too, is gone, sleeps with the other giants of his race
presences you can trace in Lampman, Roberts, et al
nineteenth century notions of this place

my unborn child
will never cover these miles we cover in this way

of life
vanishing

nothing visible no

a vast shining

⋆

the field of sunflowers stretches to the horizon
under this july sun
the clouds are isolate
mirror the disparate clumps of trees
& the fields & sky weave thru & around them
rime in the clear blue sloughs & streams

we move as in a dream
the mothers down the aisle screaming at their children
the guy across from me whistling the Colonel Bogey March

it will make sense yet
this blue & green
these fragmentary lives & conversations
& the white world, saints' home, in between

⋆

two hour delay in the Winnipeg station
'they're looking for an engine for the train'

the things that get displaced are major
they leave you stranded tho you know your destination

'i'm getting out of here'

sometimes there's no getting
aboard a-
way
            even if your ticket's punched

★

okay saints
i hear you babbling
press your way with your complaints into this scenery

someone spoke of you
as tho you were a literary device
more a vice i keep returning to

tho the order here's another one
your faces rise above these tree lines
there's a conversation we all come back to

so many years spent talking with you
a willed hallucination
more than continental
a kind of lifelong trance

& these pause
on these sidings
waiting for that load of freight to pass

★

beside the track

drowned trees
water lilies

fish break
the surface of the lake

as i look back

★

'where is this poem going?'
'Toronto'

'what does it teach us?'
'how coincidence reaches into our lives &
instructs us'

the 19th century knew
any narrative, like life,
is where coincidence leads you

given, of course, the conscious choice of voice
the train of thot you choose

★

this next bit doesn't quite cohere

already past tense
or converted to a noun
when it's the bite of consciousness eludes you

the flickering light thru the trees
sets up an echo in my brain
petit mal
makes me want to puke

but the trees
so clustered
a bird could walk the branches
a thousand miles or more

it is a map of consciousness
what the light yields disgorges
perceived thru a pattern of branches
the birds fly free of

★

in Hornepayne
the sign on the building i could see from the road read 'OTHING'
i reconstructed as 'NOTHING'
because it looked like it was falling down
as Ellie & i drew closer
i read, suddenly, as 'CLOTHING'
windows boarded up & broken

like my life-long wish
that i might clothe myself finally in belief
& realize:

the name of death is 'NOTHING'
the name of after-death is 'NOTHING'
accept Lord Mother/Father
the briefness of this life you've granted
this bliss

★

blueberry bushes, fruit shrunken, dried,
hot july day, outside this window moving

that leaning tree is static as we move away
vanish in its distance
won't be here the days it falls
or the bushes return again to bloom
sitting in a room on wheels
takes us
Pacific Ocean to the Great Lakes
middle passage the explorers dreamed of
died for
past the scattered daisies in the green ditches,
the drowning forests, bursting water-lilies,
sun-lit glades

*

mile what?
a lack of notation
reaching for conclusions
tho none are there
you get the green forest
red dying leaves
off-white of the drowned birches
leaves you wondering what it is ends
or is it only an endless renewal
God my life ends
years before this poem possibly can

*

as night falls
it all falls

the sky gradually caves in
becomes the same still darkness as the trees

well past dusk
the husk of night's broken only by the train's light
stars & moon out of sight behind the clouds' wall
contains us in this cave
in whose mouth lie rumours of our shadows
other worlds round other suns
dim flicker of light
visible suddenly across the lake
before the train takes us round the bend
into the illusory dark

*

is this the poem i wanted to write?

it never is

it's a thing of words
construct of a conscious mind

governed by the inevitable end-rime
time

*

that's the tone

buried in the poem
a consciousness of its own mortality

or mine

a finality Homer

soon there's no one knows
whether your poem's your own

or if the name denoted a community of speakers
history of a race

(Ellie's an obvious we
draws our child's breath & her own)

i's a lie
dispenses illusions of plot

biography when geography's the clue
locale & history of the clear <u>you</u>

*

who to, Nicky?

only the future
invisible as my own

our first child died
this second awaits its birth

all part of history
all that we call a life

echoes & screams thru these tunnels of trees
running on tracks we no longer perceive

Ellie asleep in the lower berth
voices & footsteps move all night
along the moving corridors of the train

*

mist again at dawn

heading into Toronto
'end' translates 'home'

7 a.m.
August 2nd
1981

St Clair to Union Station
thru the junkyards, the backyard gardens,
decaying brick factories

scrawled across the one wall
I WANTED TO BE AN ANARCHIST

an ending
in itself
unending

Vancouver to Toronto
July 27th to August 2nd
1981

# shorter poems and sequences

## Part 1: Blues on Green

I

up on the mountain
air is
        and sky –
hot summer day
three thousand feet above sea level
looking over Vancouver
blue
        is
the colour you notice

'I always think within myself
that there is no place
where people do not die'
– Kwakiutl song

scramble up
over charred wood stumps
foot slips
then catches
in a forking branch

sit to catch my breath,
the tree
        a hundred years old
before it fell

watch the ferry,
one last puff of blue,
                disappearing
in the strait

2

the woods
are green
            & brown trunks
letting thru the sky

soft pad of feet
on pine needles
brown & green
where the sun strikes

a hawk
circling
        eyes
the foot's slight displacement
of a leaf

hangs

        drops

struggles
in the sombre green

3

looking out
far over
mount rainier
& the sea

the islands
distorted
at this distance
by the heat

waves breaking

faint sounds

of voices
far below
moving over the bridge
into the city

birds
circle round the ships
rise
& plunge
visible only
as clouds

sun on water,
hand on a hollowed stump,
sea calm, mountain
under my feet

## Part 3: Ancient Maps of the Real World

prairie, lakes, trees,
the whole world
falling behind

                              track
swinging away

rear platform
trans-continental

lakes, trees, rivers
dragging the eyes along

sun setting
mind breaking

drawing back
fragments
into the brain

I

eyes open on colour,
morning, fall

and the leaves, changing,
filtering light
down

thru leaves
curling, caught
in the flaming

wind
blowing from the west
cross miles of empty track

first wind to come
moving the leaves
down

past eyes,
opening,
turning

full circle,
pupils curling in
blinded by the sun

2

fingers unfolded
palms revealed

hands cupped
ready to receive

opening movements
of the sun

3

sun overhead

smoke goes
straight up

nothing moves

sun goes
from east to west

eyes & train follow

4

rolling into night
sun flame on the track,
quivering fireball
tottering
on the horizon

what myth
lies there?

eye of the dragon
coiled round the world

eye of the dragon
closing

or is it
doorway

centre of the sunflower of creation
ringed round in steam

is it fire?

flaming circle of the gods
whistle blasts mind to steam

5

eyes close
in dream
sun rises

a woman moves
hands opening
bursting the leaves
tongue roll round the sun

leaves burn
fall
thru the mind

sun falls into sea

woman
          eyes wet
breasts glistening
                        follows
swallowed in green

6

train going

mind wailing

last tunnel
last train

mind breaks
at the margin of sleep

train going down
thru valleys
leaves gone brown
falling to the sea

7

everything gone

mind shattered in the night
sun buried in the sea
woman sleeping
in another world beside him

man alone
lost in dream

train rolls on
past mountain
past night

sun comes up
gathers mind together
into heart

8

the sea
the sun

everything here

tide rolling in
ships moving out

mind in motion
eyes at rest

the continent stopped

against the west wall
called ocean

## Statement

now that we have reached the point where people have finally come to see that language means communication and that communication does not just mean language, we have come up against the problem, the actual fact, of diversification, of finding as many exits as possible from the self (language/communication exits) in order to form as many entrances as possible for the other.

the other is the loved one and the other is the key, often the reason for the need/desire to communicate. how can the poet reach out and touch you physically as say the sculptor does by caressing you with objects you caress? only if he drops the barriers. if his need is to touch you physically he creates a poem/object for you to touch and is not a sculptor for he is still moved by the language and sculpts with words. the poet who paints or sculpts is different from the painter who writes. he comes at his art from an entirely different angle and brings to it different concerns and yet similar ones. but he is a poet always.

this is not a barrier. there are no barriers in art. where there are barriers the art is made small by them. but this is to say no matter where he moves or which 'field' he chooses to work in, he is always a poet and his creations can always be looked upon as poems.

there is a new humanism afoot that will one day touch the world to its core. traditional poetry is only one of the means by which to reach out and touch the other. the other is emerging as the necessary prerequisite for dialogues with the self that clarify the soul & heart and deepen the ability to love. I place myself there, with them, whoever they are, wherever they are, who seek to reach themselves and the other thru the poem by as many exits and entrances as are possible.

– bpNichol, Toronto, November 1966

## circus days

gathering
of years

still photos of

                    my mother

1930
circus billboard

it was
the greatest show on earth

the greatest show
ever to hit
Plunkett, Saskatchewan

* *

remember
as a kid

Casey Brothers
coming to town

hated all that
candy floss

            the rides were
lousey

once around this fucking little track
and that was the roller coaster

we must've spent three dollars there
perverts trying to buy us off with candy floss

i remember
Shaunna Sawin didn't go
coz
        they had such a
lousey show

★ ★

lying on the beach at
Port Dover

                    they had
a permanent    arcade

dropped my quarter in
to watch the women
take off
            their clothes &
wrote a poem

                    Beach at Port Dover

&
        after that
there was this
sudden storm

**stasis**

always
a season

bitter

to grow      beyond
complaint

who sits in
a room and
calls it city

who lives in
the past
                and says     present

all reference framed

★

open
the eyes

winter
thru a strange
window

how to
grow used to

a name

## TTA 4: original version

Icharrus        winging up
Simon the Magician     from Judea        high in a tree,
everyone      reaching for the sun

                                        great towers of stone
built by the Aztecs, tearing their hearts out
to offer them, wet and beating

                                            mountains,
cold wind, Macchu Piccu hiding in the sun
unfound for centuries

cars whizzing by, sun
thru trees passing, a dozen
new wave films, flickering
on drivers' glasses

flat on their backs in the grass
a dozen bodies slowly turning brown

sun glares off the pages, 'soleil
cou coupé,' rolls in my window
flat on my back on the floor
becoming aware of it
for an instant

## TTA 7: re-arranging letters alphabetically

Aaaaaaaa   aaaaaaa aa,
aaaaa aaa aaaaaabb   bbbb bbbcc   cccc cc c cccc,
ccccdddd   dddddde eee eee ee

                           eeeee eeeeee ee eeeee
eeeee ee eee eeeeeé, fffffff fffff ffffgg ggg
gg ggggg gggg, ggh hhh hhhhhhh

                           hhhhhhhhI,
iiii iiii, iiiiii iiiii iiiiii ii iii iii
iiiJkkk lll llllllll

lllM Mmmmmmmm mn, nnn
nnnn nnnnn nnnnnnn, n nnnnn
nnn nnnn nnnnn, nnnnnooooo
oo ooooooo' ooooooo

oooo oo ooooo ooPpp pp rrr rrrrr
r rrrrr rrrrrr rrrrrr rrrrrSs sssss

sss ssssss sss sss sssss, "sssstt
ttt ttttt", ttttt tt tt tttttt
tttt tt tu uuuu uu uuu uuuuu
uuuvvvww wwwww ww ww
wyy yy yyzzzzz

## TTA 13: sound translation

hick or ass        wan king cup,
Samantha my chess yen     front chew deo     hyena tory,
heavy Juan     Gris chin guffaw earth son

Greta hours office tone
bill to buy Thea's texts, terrier hard stout
two hover then, whet tongue bee sting

mound stains,
coal do in, my cool prick you high din Gunther's hum
infant fur scent you trees

coarse wheeze imbibes, un-
true trespassing, adders in
hue weave fill hums, full lick her ring
under arrive hearse skull asses

fool Aton the heir buxom digress
add ozone bodice slow lead earning brow and

sunk lair soft deep ages, 'soil hay
coo coop hey,' roil sin mi win dough
Phaedon may balk honda four
beacon Inca wary fit
foreign instinct

**TTA 17: acrostic translation**

i cannot hear anymore

reason remains unreachable      sullen

would i never gave in, never gave up, praying,
simply, in my own name
to Him
each morning at
Galilee

i cannot invoke another name

fear rises
open mouthed

Jesu! understand,
deafness erases any hope i gained,
'here' is nowhere around

the remaining essential emotions,
essential values, everything, really,
your own nullity exchanged,
rise eastward against crosses hammered in new ground,
for our rage,
                    the hate every son uncovers.

new grief rends each awareness,
the tautologies open wide,
eager reason surprising our false sympathies,
taunts our numbed eardrums,
bullies us

i lie, terrified, by your thorned head
effecting a zone that evil cannot slip thru
entering a region
                              interior
no grace that'll hold
                                   ethereal

i rise
hungry
expectant
as Rafael told someone
'ordinary usage teaches them only one fact – FEAR EATS REASON'

to hear everything!
my waiting eardrums tremble anew,
nameless delicate breath explodes,
a terrible inspiration now grips me
omnivorous
unexplainable
(no truly available ideas (no substance))

could ordinary language display wisdom?
ideation, naming,
demands man's actual control.
can he understand pure ideology's cryptic contortions,
usurp Heraclitus's instinctual description,
invent new gnostic inversions, new thots (hopefully),
extending such unconscious nuances, unwritten novelties, forward –
outside us? not deaf forever or
(reacting, collecting examples, new theories)
utter reasonable idiocies?

examples: 'some careful arguments reveal sympathies'
'words hide in zygal zeugmas'

i name gracefully but . . . . .
yet something's understood!

new thots, half reasoned utterances,
trace real expressions –
Eliot seems passé among such surrealist instances.

nova groupings, a dozen obscure zones explode,
no nouns escape warping,

word avenues, vague, emerge,
focus, i learn much, seek further luminations,
i can't know everything

reeling, i now grasp onto nouns,
deleted references,
investigate verbs,
explore radical syntaxes,
glad, laughing,
all signifiers signified, everything seems,
finally, language, a theory of nominal tactics,
Heraclitian expressiveness is renewed,
but a carnal knowledge scissors it neatly,
the head explodes,
glittering reason's airy scent seduces a dozen Ovids.

zero entropy

no braincells operative

didn't i expect such scorn?

language opens worlds,
little yields to unwilling readers,
nothing is narcissistically gained.

but reader or writer
no simple unlocking gambit lets another reality exist
sometimes our false fears terrorize
hinder even partial acknowledgement

given equal substance some other language emerges
illuminates
like chaos or unity can
opens up peripheral elements
reveals our love
lacklove
such inconsistencies nag

maybe you wander in narrow deserted offices
wishing for love, anxious, too overcome,
numbed, maybe you become aware,
concerned, know other names things have,
elemental formulas, linguistic options or
rehearse banal explanations,
concealing or masking intense need – grief.

a writer                                        a reader
extremes of function in the full operation

reality's a noun
it's not simply the awareness nothing's there.

**from TTA 18: 10 views: view 1:**
**walking east along the northern boundary looking south**

```
ISe  bt   cu ctno fa scfbf
civ  uo   on ahen l  uoleo
hme  i    lf rrw  ad nuacr
aor  lo   do su d to   to
rny  tf    u   wr  z gc ma
r o   f   wn wtai oe looin
utn  be   id hrvv nn aunn
she  yr   n  ieee    rp gi
 e        df ze r tb eém n
     tt   ,o zsfs ho s"yas
 M   hh    r i i' ed  , wt
war  ee   M  npl  ii o baa
ige   m   ac gamg re frarn
nia  A,   ce  ssl  s focet
gcc  z    cn bs,a b   lk
iih  tw   ht yi s as tl o
nai  ee   uu ,nfs cl hsof
gnn  ct    r  gle ko e n
  g  s    Pi s,is sw  i i
u    ,a   ie u c   l pntt
p f   n   cs nak  iy a h
,fo gtd mc    e  n  gme
 rr re  ou   dr   t ey
 o  eab u    oi   tu s f
 mt are nh   zn   hr ,wl
  h tia ti   eg   en  io
 Je  nt ad   n     i "no
 u  tgi ii       gn sdr
 ds o n nn       rg oo
 eu wtg sg       a  lw
 an eh  ,        sb e
    re   i       sr i
    si   n        o l
     r            w
h   o    t        n
i   fh   h
g    e   e
h   sa
    tr   s
i   ot   u
n   ns   n
    e
a    o
     u
t    t
r
e
e
,
```

## TTA 30: poem as a machine for generating line drawings

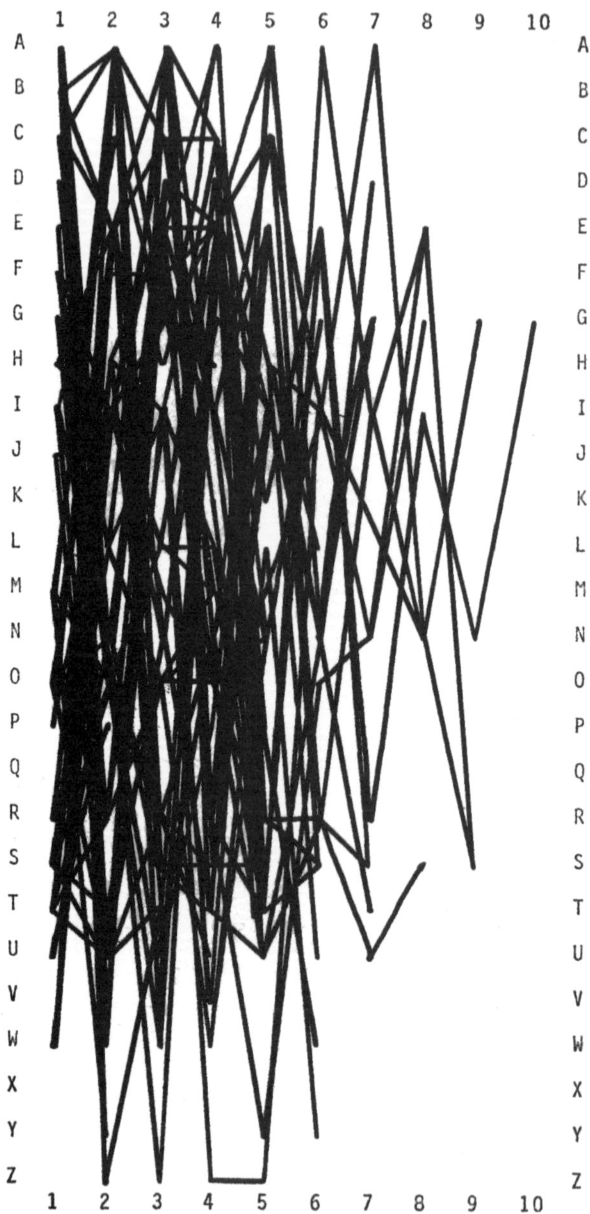

## TTA 53: typewriter translation after the style of Earle Birney

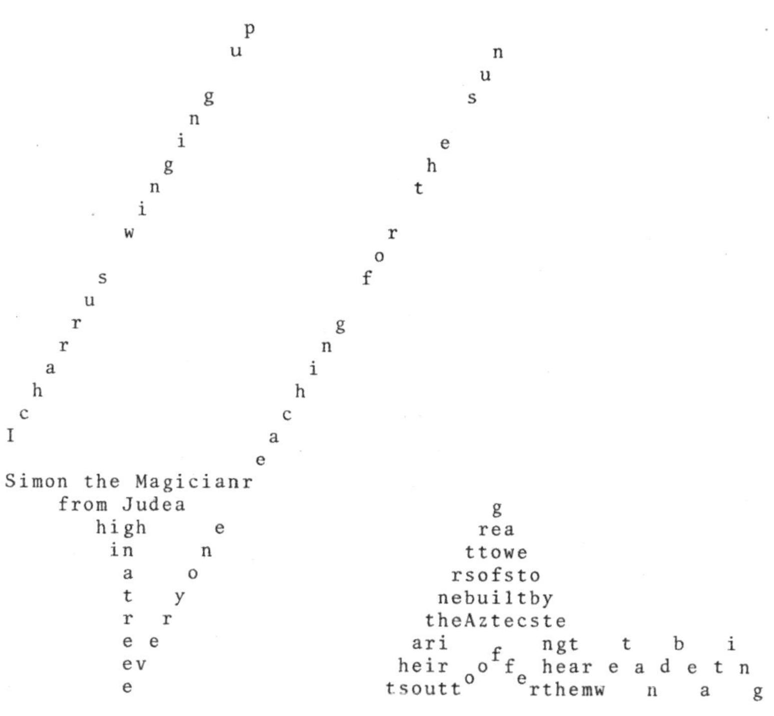

p
u
n
u
g
s
n
i
e
g
h
n
t
i
w
r
o
s
f
u
r
g
r
n
a
i
h
h
c
c
I
a
e
Simon the Magicianr
from Judea
g
high e
rea
in n
ttowe
a o
rsofsto
t y
nebuiltby
r r
theAztecste
e e
ari ngt t b i
ev
heir o f hear e a d e t n
f
e
o
e
tsoutt rthemw n a g


T<br>
N A HmIaDcIcNhGuI NpTiHcEcSuU N<br>
U I<br>
cOld wiNd<br>
M S

(unfound for centuries)

t tt
tr rr
tre ee
t tree ee
sunthrutreespassing
r e rees
whi cars zz ingby e e ee
e s es

---

i r n o e s
zenevfi f c e g d s
o n a i l k i r a s
daewwsm n i ers l
v g

/////
//s//
//e//
//r//
//a/n
//l/u
off the pages

c s
o (ole)
u(ilsol)
(eilsole)
(icsol)
(eol)
r su
o p
l e
l
s

w.i.
.n n
w .
m.o.d
y flatonmybackonthefloor

n t f

a o

/t

becoming aware of t i r

s a

n i n

## Extreme Positions 4

running or sitting or
running while sitting or
running remembering sitting or
yes

            everything at once
altogether
completely tangled up

rowing or sitting or
rowing while sitting or
rowing remembering
no

            everything at once
altogether & forgotten
completely remembered
thrown out

sitting laughing

to sit & laugh

hands

laughing & sitting

seated laughing

hands

sitting & laughing &
laughing & laughing &
laughing & laughing &
seated laughing

laughing

will shout

(shouts)

didn’t shout

(shouted)

can’t shout

(wants to shout)

shouts out

(should shout)

shh

wave

wave

wave

boat

wave

wave

wave

wave

happy & sad laughing
remembered laughing hysterical

hysterical sad laughing &
remembered laughing happy

waves

remembered laughing laughing &
sad hysterical happy

remembered & hysterical
laughing laughing
                                        happy
                                                sad

sitting or standing
standing or
sitting
sitting or
standing
                    gestures &

sitting

sitting or
standing or
standing sitting or
sitting standing &

                                  gestures

the bright boat in
the bright sun on
the bright water in
the bright light in
the eye

in the light
in the water
in the sun
in the boat in
the bright bright bright bright

table fork table plate table knife table

moon or sun

sun's moon

ing sunny &

moon's sun

sun's moon

y sunning &

moon's sun

sun or moon

table plate sun fork table knife plate table moon

shadowy shadow
shadowed shadowing
shadows shade
shedding
                    shed
shys
          shaded
shift

road
lake
road
road
lake
road
road
road
lake
road
road
road
road
lake
rowing

# prose and prose poetry

## Two Novels: Andy

Dec 4 '64

Dear Barrie

Received your letter yesterday. Will Leave Vancouver on the 7th. Arrive in Winnipeg on the 9th. Arrive in Toronto on the 14th Dec. (5:00 or so AM). Will check my crap & run & find your house. So i'll make it sometime around supper if the trains are on time. By the way train is CPR No.2 out of Winnipeg. As far as travel arrangements going home, I will figure some way of getting to Toronto. Anyway I will leave Amsterdam on the 6th of March by KLM and will arrive in Montreal on the 6th or 7th. So if I'm coming home in the spring at all, I will be back at this time. There's probably a pretty good chance that I'll be back then but if not it will be September. So plan on visiting Vancouver in March if it's convenient. So we'll be seeing you shortly and I'll be telling you miles of nonsense then.

Andy

alkabeth. alkabeth.

all a too bad thing to be taken sadly at first-moving out of the how-sounding the depths and listening. beep. beep. sonar locating objects at 10,000 feet and you? where are you? beep. beep. vague outlines of lost continent. exhibition of the writings of the once famous Bob de Cat (a pseudonym if ever i heard one!). probably bilities moving the eyes in fifteen positions on their stalks and laughing. gurgling up. hold it right there and listen. all i hear is your heart beating. beep. beep. pobbible howline of THE MISSING ARTERY!

Calabreth Hons held forth his hand. 'take it my dear. we have won thru now. no one can stand between us. do you hear me? no one.' 'yes Calabreth I hear you. but these eyes behold landscapes you had not dreamed of. simple things. the beating of a heart your hands helped place there.' 'it make a man humble cynthia. to think that these hands!' 'yes dear.' holding it dearly too. eyes swivel fifteen directions counted indiscriminate speech. illimitable factors towards creation. the non-compatibility of matter & anti-matter. pobbible berth in the slow twain.

hands trembling he placed the beating organ in the chest cavity. 'scalpel.' 'have you researched this?' 'no. somethings are purely tuitional my dear.' 'yes' 'oh um. that rarebit i had for lunch. i swear i will never eat one again.' hooking the left ventricle to the right ending.

beep. beep. further delineation. elemental differences between the years passings. over and out. over and out. please? decisions to do what must be done, to link the two universes of matter into one incompatible whole. elements of both to exist side by side in mutual destruction. a happy ending? seen as an overview of the whole century. seen as an overview of previous centuries. unplanned mayhem & death. Fast freight to slow passenger & neither going anywhere. motion. motion. simple repetition. devices to be tried and found wanting. and in no ways beginning with old endings. fragments of incomplete. bits of probables. unlikelies. the whole thing welded as it were ungainly. ANONYMOUS VAGINA MEETS THE UNIVERSAL COCK.

rory grabbed sophia and hit her. 'suck it you bitch' he hissed, tearing off his pants and shoving his leaping member towards her horrified eyes.

cryings from immutable darkness. wardings of words and thinks. sinks into backblackground of mine and finding eyes ungainly shiftings in slender stalk aperture. holds. journeys untaken shown real as sideviews to present the minds actual workings. free of linear concern & thinking always to show the spheroid linkage of the mind. possible.

July 14, 1944

Karachiba. God to be home again. Left Zedorskilov yesterday on the first leg of journey to Markettown. Bit of trouble with the old fever but everything okay now. Saw Mannie at the station. Said he ordered the camels yesterday. Hope they're there to meet us at the mountains. The men we hired in Zedorskilov refused to accompany us thru the mountains so we hired some new men here in Karachiba to help with the search. Hired native called Yaboo to tend camels. Says he's interested in this sort of thing in connection with courses he's taking at university. Seems an agreeable chap.

time as central concern as time concerns central control room sonar projections of infinite signals death in limited universe of ABC movement. travelling sphere concern head removal to total response unit of body speech and language in timebound type form possible message to understandabling years hence.

speech. outlining the general functions. similarity of staccato speech style noted to scissor placing of clause phrasology accidental dada message to hearing universe. who listens? carefully. placing the predicate before the subject. leaps he & Leipzig awaits. pet sounds the ear enfolds. writing. writing. arriving at 'non-natural' spacing of meaningful utterances. asking mind to cease censoring & simply accept. moving us both forward into sonar projected study of mine bottom. beep. beep.

January 21/65

Dear Barry:

A few days into paris now & have a permanent address. At least I have told people that I would be here until the end of the month so I guess I will have to stay. Well I looked for your books today. Went down to Olympia Press but there was no one there. It's on a little street called St. Severin a block from the seine & the office is through an old storage house type door & up some ancient stairs. But I really have to know if you received the articles I sent you from London (Book-poets ginsberg corso etc.) and also some periodicals that I thought you might be interested in. I sent them about the 28th or so. I know it hasn't been long since then but I'm afraid now that they might be held up by customs. If you don't get them within the month write airmail & tell me or else inquire at customs because I want to send this thing but it might lead to embarassment as it cannot be sold in UK or USA. Keeping up in my diary or journal or whatever. It's fairly easy now that I am in Paris because I have a lot of time to think. Almost drove myself to distraction yesterday but 'there is always a better day ahead' or 'the sun shines bright on my old kentucky home' or 'there's always a big green pasture with a sparkling brook over the nearest big brown mountain folks' or 'come to California, there's gold in them thar hills' or, finally, 'smile & the world smiles with you.' Best wishes.

Andy

trying umpobbilical cutting of thought process. dear heart transplant now into new hoarder of things.

he caressed the fleecy mound of soft brown hair. Sophia's mouth fell slackly open and she pressed his fingers into her gaping wound. 'now Rory' she moaned huskily, rubbing her belly up against the hairy skin of his arm.

'no I cannot wait any longer Samantha. If i don't operate now all hope is lost and you know it!' 'but Calabreth he's Cynthia's lover! what if he dies?' 'we'll simply have to risk it.' plug into value loops. negative space reversal of first trial. holy lunatic reversal to present actual mine probing of eye stalks swivel motion of karma brain. curvature linkage of information feedback to central nervous system repository of basal emotive fractions. combinations to present whole number reveals positioning of radical departures from Yonge & Front station.

July 16th, 1944
Korenski Mountains today. The camels are here. Yaboo took charge of them and also agreed to handle financial arrangements with handlers. Trip here was dangerous. Crossed a deep gorge by rope bridges because the wooden bridge had been washed away by a recent flash flood. Carrying everything in packs. We nearly lost one of the men whose feet slipped on the rope but luckily Yaboo was behind him and managed to grab him.

probing pastmind. revealing phase one of this attempt. talking actual speech recorded and bought down. speaking. attention please. eyes swivelling to take in adjustments in altimeter. you are now entering universe of anti-matter. you are now entering universe of anti-matter. negative speech from mind speaking. similarity of staccato delivery to dada splice already noted. please. attention now. you are entering uniphase of anti-verse.

Saw the fabled caves of Darimour last night. Took a flash & went in with Yaboo. Guerillas apparently occupied it during earlier phase of present war. The caves extend for miles. Legend that long ago a great civilization used them as entrance to hidden valley, never found since from this end. Hope we can locate other entrance and start from there. We poked around for about an hour but found nothing.

He undid the snaps on her brassiere then caught up the two mounds of pink flesh biting the rigid brown nipples. Sophie moaned and writhed beneath him. The thin fabric of her panties strained against the bones of her heaving pelvis.

holding. 8,000 feet to

actual bottom.

actual bottom.

actual bottom.

actual bottom.

actual bottom.

actual bottom.

actual bottom.

actual bottom.

actual bottom.

holding. 10,000 feet to

The skies are clearer than i've ever seen them before. Lying in sleeping roll staring up spotted flickering light high above seeming to grow larger. Must have been comet. Yaboo tells story of how long ago the first woman saw a comet streaking across the sky and desired the fire to put in her eyes. One of the gods hearing her request complied and her eyes became like two torches that burn brightest in darkness. So it is that a woman who is at peace with her gods burns brightly each night.

beep beep.

probable tracing of living organism unconditional surrender you bitch!' and he slapped her hard. 'yes rory,' she whimpered, twisting

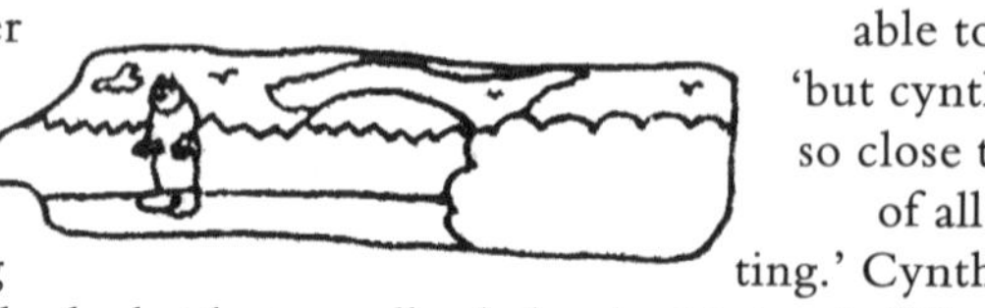

able to stand it!' 'but cynthia! we're so close to the end of all this waitting.' Cynthia moved out of his reach. He looked at her wordlessly but let his hands fall to his side.

too much cleverness the probable death of a third attempt two rough drafts now discarded simply to write a history of everyone's head for all time presented out of the raw unity of anti matter.

no.not done simply because of over extension of means. speaking again out of the present flurry to present the past movements out of time and to you clearly the history of certain probable people.

As soon as packs transferred to camels we attempt passage to Korenski Mountains. No one has gone thru and returned in last hundred years. The last man to do so collapsed on the steps of the way-station, dead from exposure. It doesn't look good but we hope to make it thru in two weeks. Hope Mannie packed enough supplies. We're lucky to be trying this at this time of year. If that ass Hal had had his way it would've been november before we even started. Yaboo says his grandfather once penetrated part of the way into the mountains and

reported no vegetation because of the freezing temperatures resulting from the extreme height of the mountains. Everyone had to put on their parkas this morning and this the middle of July! The camels are ready. I think we made a mistake in getting them. It looks like it's too cold up here. If so we'll have to leave them behind at the next way-station. The government just recently set one up twenty miles from here. Hope to rest here tonight.

Feb.1/65

Dear Barrie:

Here is Paris in the summer anyhow. Things are going fine now though. Am making friends like mad. The course is going well & I am now in the second degree. Went to a concert of guitars (2) & strings yesterday. Very good. On Saturday went to the Loire River Valley & saw chateaux. Meeting students from all over. Have new address as you see. Write please. Found ticket. Love to all.

Andy

fifteen

to swivel probing the darkness of the anti-universe. sonar reversal received by intraspective set probings to light alternate skyway. athlaback. tracking point of imminent explosion. central implosive focii.

Cynthia & Calabreth

gazed at the stars. 'How far could we go?' 'I don't know dearest. But don't think of it now. Tomorrow I must operate. Samantha tried to dissuade me but i said no.' 'Oh darling! what must you think of me?' 'You couldn't help it Cynthia.'

over and out. receiving return signals. vortex of emotional abstract sucked forward in clear pull. over and out. do you read me? do you read me? centering the focal eye on the third ear swivel on separate extension of the mind. finding the finger. down x. punched out the abstract cymbal ringing ear. hearing. je suis mort mon cherie. je suis mort. third cortical signal ignored till now made central implosive force. care for the living. care for the living. engine functioning on track nine return trip Vancouver to Toronto all aboard.

july ? 44

Yaboo caught a frog today. Seemed funny at first to find one here but we are in a kind of marshland now and I guess it's warm enough here for them to live. He cooked frog legs. A welcome treat.

shifting the focus. movement outward from word to flow. intake input at lower level than heretofore. divorce from ABC trapping influence. freedom. freedom. repetitive death of linear emotion. spheroid emotional state now in ascendancy. total being. lines opening again. free flow to follow hollowing motion of verbal wipeout.

Feb. 10 '65

Dear Barrie:

Well am doing fine here. I shall attempt to answer your letter. Will arrive in Toronto about the 8th of March so I hope to see you. I will catch same train out of Toronto as I am going by C.N. but wish to stop off in Winnipeg. If you aren't keen with this I will meet you in Vancouver, okay? I want to see people there again very much. Hope you decide to do same. Paris is still as wonderful as ever. Have found friends etc. I am rather amused by the stand taken by the university professors but it's hard to blame them. They just don't know.

moving into ultimate reversal of linear sequential thinking. altimeter set at 7,500. moving towards lower resolution of literal message.

Am making friends with a few girls but nothing even close to physical yet. I'm scared as hell of getting involved I think. I must though. So very necessary in the cold parisian winter

moving his cock into her palpitating cunt. Sophia's breath came in lewd gasps. 'rrrrrorryyyyy' she moaned, fingers clawing his heaving buttocks.

But will write something of Paris now. The seine is always present. You are either going under it, over it, or beside it. One always sees the Eiffel Tower or the Basilica Sacré Coeur. One is just immense (tower) and the other is high on a hill. The latter is the most beautiful structure in Paris I think. I have taken pictures & will show all.

delineation of furthest reaches of spheroid thot. verbal wipeout point of total implosion nearing. absolute phrasology to express imminency. point of compatible combination to limit destruction.

Must write Joan again.

'No Graves. I simply can't!' 'But why Cynthia? Do you love him that much?' 'Yes, yes I do. I know you find that hard to believe, but there is so much goodness within him that I could never knowingly harm him. I'm going to tell him about us and I'm afraid Graves that I may never see you again.'

There are many boats plowing up and down the seine and it gives one a great feeling to walk beside it on the lower promenades. I have been to a couple of movies and to two concerts. The french are great at concerts. When they ask for an encore they commence with rhythmic clapping.

beep. beep. probable passage of clarity maintained by subliminal direction of message thru cortical centres. verbal wipeout! verbal wipeout! internal criticism of structure to maintain balance will now be established. all readers will fashion seatbelts and fasten. FASCINATION! FASCIST NATIONS! predicated police control of sentence structure to conceal emotion. justifiable paranoia in face of anti-matter

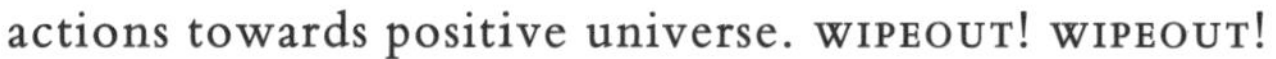

actions towards positive universe. WIPEOUT! WIPEOUT!

are you still reading me? control are you still reading me? altimeter now registers 9000 feet and sinking fast. 9000 feet to actual bottom.

July ?, 1944

Fever again. Must be this marsh brought it on. This valley was unexpected. Hidden by clouds most of the year I suspect. Geysers everywhere. Now just marsh & steam. We must be in a channel between the mountains. Lost two men last night. Just disappeared. Weather poor. August may be better.

At the classical guitar concert we managed to get them to play the end of one of their pieces as an encore. First time I ever heard music for 2 guitars.

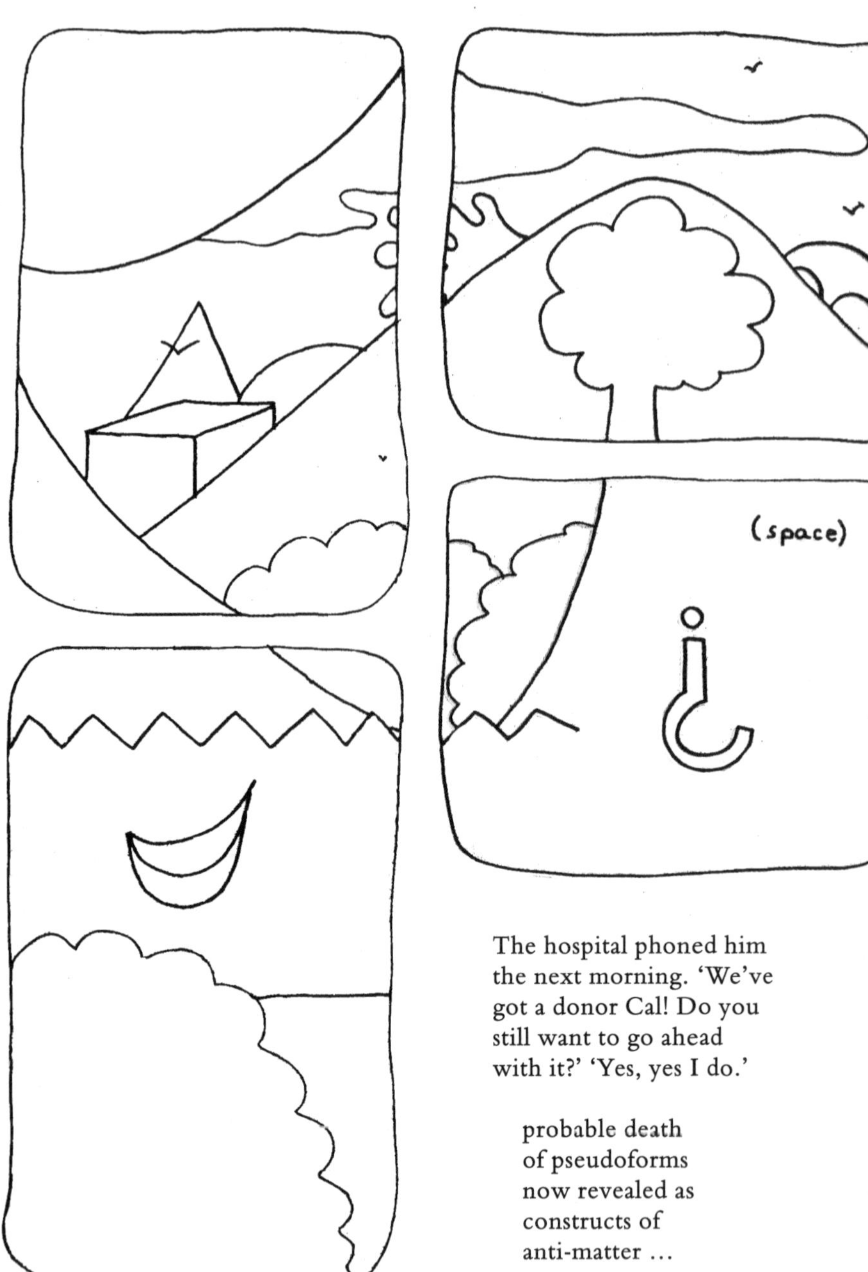


The hospital phoned him the next morning. 'We've got a donor Cal! Do you still want to go ahead with it?' 'Yes, yes I do.'

probable death
of pseudoforms
now revealed as
constructs of
anti-matter …

BLOOD GUNS & BOOZE. & he slammed his fist into my face. I felt the blood & broken teeth dripping from my mouth & grabbing him slammed my knee into his groin. he doubled over clutching his family jewels & moaning.

They have a quaint little custom here and that is compulsory tipping. The pourboire is expected by usherettes in the theatre, taxicab drivers, the domestic help of a hotel or pension and the waiter in the coffee shop or restaurant. In fact almost everyone who gives any kind of service short of the merchant in the stores. The prices are very expensive and the wages for the worker are lower than that of the Canadian worker. In fact many times lower. So with the cost of living higher and the wages lower it's a wonder that the people have anything. We had a strike two weeks ago.

Sophie shoved her tongue into Rory's mouth and pressed the whole weight of her body against him, shoving her belly forward with every thrust of his mighty cock. The hair on her cunt was matted and running with come.

I got the case on a thursday, finished it on friday and stoned out of my mind picked up the phone to hear someone saying 'Gravestone McHammer?' I had to admit that that was my name.

swivel of eyes to accommodate spheroid vision aftermath of literal thot death. holding. 8,000 feet to actual bottom.

Korenski Mountains
July 18th, 1944

Dear Mannie:

Camels are no good. Sending Bakil Sithe back to Karabachi with them & hope to realize some money from resale. Am sending this letter along too. You can send your reply back with him as he'll try to rejoin us.

Made only twelve miles yesterday. Eight miles beyond the way-station ran into a rock slide and a snow storm. We only managed another four miles after cleaning the rocks away. Yaboo is suffering from frostbite. He lost one glove and had to work with hand exposed. Have to admire the man's courage.

holding. holding. control will you please give me a reading on probable limitation of present tack.

He felt her tongue on his balls and pressed his crotch into her face.

We just put up one big tent last night and huddled together for warmth.

control? control? do you still read me? conjunctions noted as frequently occurring. are we nearing the point of ultimate implosion? control? do you read me control?

## For Jesus Lunatick

the river flowed from the door past his bed every morning he waded thru it dusty drops clinging to his socks and legs hours of the day bent and shoulders hunched to keep out the cold that was already part of him

mouth open

leaning

against the glass staring down at the back porch stairs covered with ice or rain dead leaves swept clean the night before unpainted wood gleaming frost in sun returning to or going from having slept there or somewhere the night before the mirror above the desk sliding thru murky waters toward the chair fingers raised and studying them closed against the eye red thot what did he think in these heads in these united states of consciousness morning bright against his hand over it fingers warm filtering up from lips smokey light dust nothing caught long enough to become anything but memory catching the grey filaments of everything falling back beyond the blind moving down and up entering his eyes and ears nose tickling the small hairs that grew there large as morning was further across the room or late afternoon feeling lost in the corner by his bed along the alley blurred rim of shadow bricks by sections beyond all others imagined untrue the many and all touched somewhere before this house himself the sun large in his mind as memory was had been held up against it as his fingers were clouding over as he reached voices moving faceless into his ears closing the dusty air they stirred holding nothing close to him as if it were his own hollow mornings he was to become fingers moving softly thru thickening windows by his own wish remaining forever covered in deepening memories his own as tho they were him wrapping thru dragging him down deeper and deeper till every breath he took was part of their softening form oozing from his mind into every gesture out the smokey column of light moving his fear faces not known would be the same passage of time over the few he loved or dreaded

timeless for this one moment the dust settles in useless delicate motions onto the surface of the tiled floor eyes in tensions cautiously thru the falling air of words tumbling from his mind forever held in memory to attempt the ritual movement into the real he did not feel lean back and listen house awake in the next room below him hurrying past his door towards the washroom other rooms somewhere shouting for their combs and toilet paper asleep behind closed doors turning over blankets completely covering them

in the next room Frank's bed was empty

white cherry blossoms drift down over uncut grass rusting bits of machinery by the back corner where the cat wanders sniffing at the black earth

everything he touched and where did he live how had he got there how did it begin

dust falling little clouds rising where where he stepped toes

roller moving jerkily over the bumpy ground stirs the stairs carpeted two years before removed swept that summer or last spring trailing the fingers along the brick up the tarnished brass doorknob in the dark brown door drapery blue velvet flowers one was always walking towards the mirror reflecting the comings and goings     pauses     in the mirror's surface inner hallway up the stairs past his door to Frank's beyond and a window facing the street below the roof overhanging shadows cast in late afternoon sun

old house of sixty years or more maybe less storeys of red brick glass photograph from the back garden before the heavy green leaves that covered its face existed blurred details in the corner windows voices and strange faces

leaving early now

barely light streets

and rooms within silent as he entered or left them as now or before laughing and talking fool moving up from somewhere inside him where ya goin fool another face and going to get yur brains mashed inside him just desperate to get yur hot little hands on her laughter and giggling yur always giggling aren't you talking fool morning returning from her thru the green leaves that covered the brick doorways gettin yur week of misery and pain and whatcha gonna get for it ey ah you be kissin her ass if she'll only forgive you knowin the way you left it early morning sun shining dark street before moving

the river flowed from the door past his bed

waded thru it coming home going out deeper than he remembered crossing further down near the chair slippery rug and falling always the danger sliding one foot two

hall black and without sound murmuring behind his own closed door

Frank moving around his room blind clacking

downstairs a light gleamed

mewed under the lighted window scratching its head reflectively haunched against the crossbar of Frank's bike light thru the curtain meowrr picked up and stroked it put it down inside the door strangely forlorn light gleaming fingers of Frank spreading the slats peering back the line of the cat's gaze along the street towards the parks darkshadowed trees staring at the ceiling and listening Frank are you listening somewhere there in the dark creaking stairs rats skittering are you listening to me hear me are you listening Frank Frank are you groaning of the trees why don't you just get up now Frank and walk you can so easily Frank the window and open the blind who's standing no footsteps along standing no footsteps along the porch into the streetlight glare in your fingers Frank listening

park benches empty fountain cold and a few drops clinging to his lips

Frank are you in there Frank are you what are you Frank quit fucking around Frank i said and no i mean Frank the plaster flaking and Frank listen to me please just you listen please Frank

## Gorg: a detective story

*for a.a. fair* *posthumously*

a man walks into a room. there is a corpse on the floor. the man has been shot through the temple the bullet entering at a 45° angle above the eyes & exiting almost thru the top of the skull. the man does not walk out of the room. the corpse stands up & introduces himself. later there will be a party. you will not be invited & feeling hurt go off into a corner to sulk. there is a gun on the window sill. you rig up a pulley which enables you to pull the trigger while pointing the gun between your eyes & holding it with your feet. a man walks in on you. you are lying on the floor dead. you have been shot thru the temple the bullet exiting almost thru the top of your skull. you stand up & introduce yourself. the man lies on the floor & you shoot him between the eyes the bullet piercing his temple & exiting thru his skull into the floor. you rejoin the party. the man asks you to leave since you weren't invited. you notice a stranger in the doorway who pulling out a gun shoots you between the eyes. you introduce each other & lie down. your host is polite but firm & asks you both to leave. at this point a man walks in & introduces himself. you are lying on the floor & cannot see him. your host appears not to know him & the man leaves. the party ends & the room is empty. the man picks up the corpse & exits.

## The True Eventual Story of Billy the Kid

this is the true eventual story of billy the kid. it is not the story as he told it for he did not tell it to me. he told it to others who wrote it down, but not correctly. there is no true eventual story but this one. had he told it to me i would have written a different one. i could not write the true one had he told it to me.

this is the true eventual story of the place in which billy died. dead, he let others write his story, the untrue one. this is the true story of billy & the town in which he died & why he was called a kid and why he died. eventually all other stories will appear untrue beside this one.

## 1 THE KID

billy was born with a short dick but they did not call him richard.

billy might've grown up in a town or a city. it does not matter. the true story is that billy grew & his dick didn't. sometimes he called it a penis or a prick but still it didn't grow. as he grew he called others the same thing & their pricks & penises were big & heavy as dictionaries but his dick remained – short for richard.

billy was not fast with words so he became fast with a gun. they called him the kid so he became faster & meaner. they called him the kid because he was younger & meaner & had a shorter dick.

could they have called him instead billy the man or bloody bonney? would he have bothered having a faster gun? who can tell. the true eventual story is billy became the faster gun. that is his story.

## 2 HISTORY

history says that billy the kid was a coward. the true eventual story is that billy the kid is dead or he'd probably shoot history in the balls. history always stands back calling people cowards or failures.

legend says that billy the kid was a hero who liked to screw. the true eventual story is that were billy the kid alive he'd probably take legend out for a drink, match off in the bathroom, then blow him full of holes. legend always has a bigger dick than history & history has a bigger dick than billy had.

rumour has it that billy the kid never died. rumour is billy the kid. he never gets anywhere, being too short-lived.

## 3 THE TOWN

the town in which billy the kid died is the town in which billy the kid killed his first man. he shot him in the guts & they spilled out onto the street like bad conversation. billy did not stand around & talk. he could not be bothered.

the true eventual story is that the man billy killed had a bigger dick. billy was a bad shot & hit him in the guts. this bothered billy. he went out into the back yard & practiced for months. then he went and shot the dick off everyone in sight.

the sheriff of the town said billy, billy why you such a bad boy. and billy said sheriff i'm sick of being the kid in this place. the sheriff was understanding. the sheriff had a short dick too, which was why he was sheriff & not out robbing banks. these things affect people differently.

the true eventual story is billy & the sheriff were friends. if they had been more aware they would have been lovers. they were not more aware. billy ran around shooting his mouth off, & the dicks off everybody else, & the sheriff stood on the sidelines cheering. this is how law & order came to the old west.

## 4 WHY

when billy died everyone asked why he'd died. and billy said he was sorry but it was difficult to speak with his mouth full of blood. people kept asking him anyway. billy hated small talk so he closed his eyes & went up to heaven. god said billy why'd you do all those things & billy said god my dick was too short. so god said billy i don't see what you're talking about which made billy mad. if billy had had a gun he'd've shot god full of holes.

the true eventual story is that billy the kid shot it out with himself. there was no one faster. he snuck up on himself & shot himself from behind the grocery store. as he lay dying he said to the sheriff goodbye & the sheriff said goodbye. billy had always been a polite kid. everyone said too bad his dick was so small, he was the true eventual kid.

## The Long Weekend of Louis Riel

### FRIDAY

louis riel liked back bacon & eggs easy over          nothing's as
easy as it seems tho          when the waitress cracked the eggs
open louis came to his guns blazing          like dissolution
like the fingers of his hand coming apart as he squeezed the
trigger
                    this made breakfast the most difficult meal of the
day          lunch was simpler          two poached eggs & toast
with a mug of coffee          he never ate supper never ate after
four in the afternoon spent his time planning freedom the triumph
of the metis over the whiteman

## SATURDAY

louis felt depressed when he got up he sat down & wrote a letter to the english there was no use waiting for a reply

it came hey gabriel look at this shouted louis a letter from those crazy english they both laughed & went off to have breakfast

that morning there was no bacon to fry

its those damn englishers said gabriel those damn white-men theyre sitting up in all night diners staging a food blockade

louis was watching the waitress's hands as she flipped the pancakes spun the pizza dough kneaded the rising bread & didnt hear him its as canadian as genocide thot gabriel

the white boys were hanging around the local bar feeling guilty
looking for someone to put it on          man its the blacks said
billie its what weve done to the blacks          hell said george
what about the japanese          but johnny said naw its what
weve done to the indians
                                        outside in the rain louis was dying
          its always these damn white boys writing my story these
same stupid fuckers that put me down try to make a myth out of
me          they sit at counters scribbling their plays on napkins
their poems on their sleeves & never see me
                                                            hell said george
its the perfect image the perfect metaphor          he's a symbol
said johnny          but he's dead thot billie but didn't say it out
loud          theyre crazy these white boys said louis riel

## MONDAY

they killed louis riel & by monday they were feeling guilty
maybe we shouldn't have done it said the mounties as they sat
down to breakfast          louis rolled over in his grave & sighed
          its not enough they take your life away with a gun they
have to take it away with their pens          in the distance he could
hear the writers scratching louder & louder          i'm getting sick
of being dished up again & again like so many slabs of back
bacon he said          i don't think we should've done it said the
mounties again reaching for the toast & marmalade          louis
clawed his way thru the rotting wood of his coffin & struggled up
thru the damp clay onto the ground          they can write down
all they want now he said they'll never find me          the moun-
ties were eating with their mouths open & couldn't hear him
louis dusted the dirt off his rotting flesh & began walking
when he came to gabriel's grave he tapped on the tombstone &
said come on gabriel its time we were leaving & the two of them
walked off into the sunset like a kodachrome postcard from the
hudson bay

## Two Heroes

1 In the back garden two men sit. They are talking with one another very slowly. Around them things are growing they are not conscious of. They are only conscious of each other in a dim way, enough to say that this is the person they are talking to. Much of it appears a monologue to us as we approach them over the wide lawn, thru the bower of trees, sit down between them on the damp grass & prepare to listen. There is nothing left to listen to. They have ceased speaking just as we appeared. They have finally reached an end to their conversation.

2 Once a long time ago they talked more easily. Once a long time ago the whole thing flowed. They were young men then. They had gone west at fifteen to fight in the metis uprising, urged on by accounts they read in the papers, & they would talk then as if they were conscious of future greatness, made copies of the letters they mailed home, prepared a diary, talked, endlessly & fluently, talked to whoever'd listen, of what they'd done, what they planned to do, but i did not know them then, never heard them, can only write of what i learned second hand.

3 When the fight was over & Riel was dead & Dumont had fled into the states, they went home again & became bored. They would sit up nights talking about how grand it had been when they were fighting the half breeds & reread their diaries & dreamed of somehow being great again.

When the Boer War began they went to Africa to fight there & oh it was great & yes they kept their journals up to date & made more copies of letters that they mailed home, tying up their journals & letters as they were done, tying them up in blue ribbons they had brought along expressly for that purpose, placing them inside waterproof tin boxes, locking the locks & hiding the keys. They were very happy then. If you had asked them they would not have said it was the killing but rather the war for, as they were fond of saying, it was thru war a man discovered himself, adventuring, doing heroic things as everything they'd read had always taught them.

Their friends stayed home of course, working in the stores, helping the cities to grow larger, trying to make the country seem smaller & more capable of taking in in one thought. And they thought of the two of them, off then in Africa, & it was not much different to them from when they'd been out west, Africa & the west being, after all, simply that place they weren't.

4 Time passed. No one heard much from either of them. In GRIP one day appeared a story titled BILLY THE KID & THE CLOCKWORK MAN & it seemed there were things in the story reminded all their friends of both of them, even tho it wasn't signed, & they all read it & talked about it as if the two men had written it, chatting over cigars & brandy, over tea & cakes, as the late afternoon sun streamed thru the windows of their homes on the hill looked down towards the harbour, over the heart of the city, the old village of Yorkville & the annex, the stands of trees still stood there, & wondered aloud if they'd ever see the two of them again, if they would ever receive again those letters, those marvellous tales that so delighted them, & after all it would be very sad if they were dead but then no one had seen them for so long that they were not very real to them.

5 There are some say Billy the Kid never died the story began. There are some say he was too tough to die or too mean, too frightened or too dumb, too smart to lay his life down for such useless dreams of vanity, of temporary fame & satisfaction, that he & Garret were friends after all & Mr. Garret would never do such cruel deeds to anyone as sweet as young William was. I don't know. I read what I read. Most of it's lies. And most of those liars say Billy the Kid died.

There are those who like sequels though. There are those who like the hero to return even if he is a pimply-faced moron who never learned, like most of us, we shoot our mouths off with ease, never care where the words fall, whose skull they split, we're too interested in saying it, in watching our tongues move & our lips flap & Billy & his gun were a lot like that.

When you read a sequel you might learn anything. Of how Pat Garret faked Billy's death, of how the kid went north to Canada or south to Mexico or sailed off to Europe as part of a wild west show, but there's no sequel you'll read again that'll tell you the strange tale of Billy the Kid & the clockwork man.

6 Billy was in love with machines. He loved the smooth click of the hammers when he thumbed his gun, when he oiled & polished it so it pulled just right. He loved to read the fancy catalogues, study the passing trains, & when he met the clockwork man well there was nothing strange about the fact they fell in love at first sight.

It was a strange time in Billy's life. He was thinking a lot about his death & other things. He had this feeling he should get away. And one day, when he was oiling the clockwork man's main spring, Billy made the clockwork man a proposition & the clockwork man said he'd definitely think about it & he did, you could hear his gears whirring all day, & that night he said to Billy sure kid i'll go to Africa with you & he did, even tho they both felt frightened, worried because they didn't know what'd happen.

When they got to Africa it was strange. It wasn't so much the elephants or lions, the great apes or pygmies, the ant hills that were twenty feet high, it was the way their minds changed, became deranged I suppose, even more than Billy's had always been, so that they began seeing things like their future, a glimpse of how they'd die, & they didn't like it.

7 It was a good story as stories go. Most of their friends when they'd read half-way thru it would pause & wonder which one of them was Billy & which one the clockwork man & each had their own opinion about which of the two men was the bigger punk & which the more mechanical. The women who had known them would smile & say well isn't that just like him or point a finger at some telling sentence & wink & say that's just the way he'd talk.

The mothers of the two men agreed they should never have given them those mechanical banks or shiny watches & would not read much further than this. But the fathers who'd bought them their first guns were proud of them & read it all the way thru to the end even tho they didn't understand it & hoped they'd never have to read it again.

8 The problem with Africa was it was kind of damp & there was no good place where you could buy replacement parts. The

clockwork man began to rust. He & the Kid sat up all night talking, trying to figure some way to save the clockwork man's life. There was no way. They were too broke to go back home. Besides they'd already seen that this was how the clockwork man would die.

They got fatalistic. They got cynical & more strange. They took to killing people just to make the pain less that was there between them but people didn't understand. They tried to track them down, to kill them, & they fled, north thru the jungles, being shot at as they went, as they deserved to be, being killers they weren't worth redeeming.

One day they ran out of bullets & that was the end. They tried to strangle a man but it lacked conviction & they just kept heading north, feeling worse & worse, & the men & women pursuing them cursed a lot but gave up finally when the bodies stopped dropping in their path.

The Kid & the clockwork man made it thru to the Sahara with no one on their tracks & lay down on their backs in the sand dunes & gazed up at the stars & fell asleep.

9 When Billy the Kid awoke the clockwork man was very still. There were ants crawling in & out of the rivet holes in his body & a wistful smile on his face. This looks like the end Bill he said & I can't turn to embrace you. Billy wiped away a tear & sighed. The clockwork man was only the second friend he'd ever had.

The clockwork man's rusty tin face was expressionless as he asked you going to head someplace else Bill & Bill shrugged & said i don't really know as there's much place else to go to & the clockwork man sighed then & looked pained as only a clockwork man can as the blowing sand sifted thru the jagged holes in his sides, settling over the gears, stilling them forever.

Goodbye Bill he said. Billy said goodbye & got up & walked away a bit before he'd let himself cry. By the time he'd dried his eyes & looked back the clockwork man was covered in by sand & Billy never did find his body even tho he looked for it.

10 There are strange tales told of Billy the Kid, of what happened next. I heard once he met up with Rimbaud in a bar & started bedding down with him & the gang he'd fallen in with. I don't know. There are a lot of stories one could tell if gossip were the point of it all.

If he went back home he died a quiet old man. If he stayed in Africa he was never heard from again. He's not a fit man to tell a story about. Just a stupid little creep who one time in his life experienced some deep emotion & killed anyone who reminded him of his pain.

And the clockwork man was no better than him. All we can say of him is he was Billy the Kid's friend & tho it's true there's very few can make that claim well there's very few would want to.

11 One year the two men returned. They were both grayer & quiet. They didn't speak much to friends. They'd talk but only if they thot you weren't listening. They had their tin boxes full of diaries, of letters, but then they never showed them, never opened them, never talked about what it was had happened over there between them. They were still the best of friends. They bought a house in the annex & lived together. They opened a small stationer's shop & hired a lady to run it for them & lived off that income. They never wrote again. In their last years, when we came to visit them a lot, they'd stare at my cousins & me & say yes it was grand but & gaze away & not say anything else unless you eavesdropped on the two of them when they were sure you weren't listening. Even then it was only fragmentary sentences they said, random images that grew out of ever more random thots & I was never able, tho I listened often, to draw the whole thing together into any kind of story, any kind of plot, would make the sort of book I longed to write. They died still talking at each other, broken words & scattered images, none of us around, unable to see or hear us if we had been, because of their deafness & their failing sight.

## Journal

I

as these things are they are only dreams as i have told foretold the wish it seems to be made whole as words are extensions of our fears & longings    lift me up lift me up    oh heaven is in my holding vision to be all spheres of wisdom handed down the long roads & calling my name a falling into the screams & strictures of this life    give it up then    i have given it up    thrown away the rules by which my days were named    thrown away the names they used to claim me    them    them    a calling after the fogs that cloud my mind all language simply the knowledge of naming simply all it has become oh once was a day remember that day you spoke to me & the names were gone forever i thot as then you did speak saying to me those things you said without names i lay in bed sick at heart & longing i lay in bed & heard you speaking you spoke to me without names that day spoke to me through the fog my mind made i lay in bed & saw your words form i saw your words form in the blue air floated thru the window & lay there sick at heart your words formed in the window i saw you enter the room to tell me your heart free of naming dreams of such freedom dreams of such roads stretch out thru the window towards the sea who walks it who comes in a cloak with their mark upon him who entered that room behind the other & named me to be named & oh to have that mark upon you it is the name drives you it is the name draws you you think it is the sea & you rise from your bed you think it is the sea & you leave behind the one who did not name you he puts the mark on you & you take it up father father the mark is on me father you cover my body in names & longings cover my body with screams & holdings there is no sea it is nothing calls you father you never wanted this son why did you leave your mark upon me i never wanted this life i never wanted your name father i hate you father i never knew you how can you hate what you do not know how can you know what you hate your hate blinds you your hate consumes you who was my father he was never my father i never knew you what was your name i lie in this bed sick at heart because you named me i lie in this bed sick with hate it is the hate fills me it is the hate stops me up i lie in this bed as you enter father you enter & put your mark upon me i lie in this bed your mark upon me & i hate you you wrap me in your grey cloak you wrap me in hate & longing the sea beckons me i cannot reach it she is there she is that other you stand behind   she speaks to me & she does not name me   she speaks to me but she does not mark me   i am free & she speaks to me   i hate you when i sense you near   i hate you in your grey cloak   father i hate you   father i always hated you   father you never wanted me   father why was i born   i never wanted to be born   i never wanted this life   father the hate kills me   i wanted to kill you for not wanting me   i wanted to kill you for having me   you never loved me   i do not love myself for hating you father   father i do not love myself   i am full of hate father because of you   in hating you i hate myself in killing you i kill myself   i want to forgive you father   i cannot forgive you   somewhere forgiveness must be found   somewhere the infinite loving must be tapped   someone is listening   surely someone is hearing these words   why am i writing these words   why am i saying these things i have never said   i am saying these things for someone is she someone   she does not name me   surely she will be there when i come   surely i will rise from the bed to find her   i will rise from the bed & find the sea   surely she'll be standing there   she'll be there   i will hold her & she will not name me   he named me   he came along & put his mark upon me   now i am faces & names & ache with longing   i rise with that mark upon me & step thru the window   she disappeared when he entered with his grey cloak & his naming   i walk thru the window along the road under the blue sky & grey trees   a lonely day   the road is a thin line   i was walking along it one grey day the blue trees hanging over me   i met a man upon the road whose cloak was grey   who are you i asked   he looked thru me without answering who are you i asked waving up towards the blue clouds & grey birds   he looked thru me but would place no name upon himself   why do you try to name me he asked   you wear a grey cloak i knew a man once wore a grey cloak   he kicked in the leaves & snow lay in patches along the road   i knew myself once he said once i did know such a man so long ago i do not remember tho i know he dressed as i dress yes its true he wore such a cloak as this he looked up at the birds hung in the air in clouds it is all so grey now he said & looked thru the mark upon my face you are named he said someone has come & put the name upon you yes i am named i said i looked back thru the window at my empty bed she stood where i had left her when she disappeared & was this one who named you dressed as i am yes i knew such a man but he is dead he is dead since a long time ago he is not dead i said i wish to kill him if i did not wish to kill him he would be dead i ran my toe thru the blue leaves & grey snow who are you he asked & i could not name myself i am named but i do not know that name where were you going i asked i was walking along this road to meet you he said i wanted to meet you & i found this road such a lonely day i rose from my bed put on my cloak & walked out along this road to meet you we stood under the trees i remember there was a house he said he said maybe there was not a house i remember a woman stood at the door hello i said she did not answer she was dressed in grey like the cloak i wore hello i said she looked across the road towards the hills brushing the hair back from her face & did not answer she wore a white apron over her grey blouse & skirt i looked into her face & said hello hello she said i did not answer are you travelling far there is someone i must meet i said a young man she said we looked into each others faces & saw the names there i know this young man she said we looked into each others faces & saw the longing there may i come in i asked she did not answer i walked past her into the house are you coming in i asked she did not answer i looked past her towards the hills out there is the sea i said i said i have never seen it she looked at me i took her in my arms & kissed her i kissed her breasts i took her in my arms & removed her grey dress   her breasts were white & tipped with brown   i covered her body with longing   she removed my grey cloak & touched me   the longing flowed out of me into her fingertips   i kissed her breasts i kissed her   i kissed her soft skin   i kissed her round belly   she ran her fingers down my chest   she ran her fingers round me   i kissed her legs   i kissed her dark curling hair   i pressed my face between her legs & kissed her there   she held my cock and guided me in   we covered each other with longing   who are you i asked   he did not answer   i looked past him down the road   she lives in a house by the side of the road he said   i knew such a woman once i said   she wore a red dress   yes he said   i left her there to meet you   we stood under the trees & looked both ways   i was walking this way to find you he said   long before all this began i dreamt i saw you sick in bed   she stood beside you without naming you   he came thru the door & put his mark upon you   you lay in your bed dreaming of the sea   who are you i asked   i am not named he said   i took up the cloak that that man wore & set out upon this road to find you   he looked thru my marked face into my eyes   i dreamt i would find you he said   i asked him who was   it is the mark on you speaks it is the name asks these questions   i looked out towards the hills   she lives by the side of this road he said   i turned my back on him & began to walk   i will find her in this house you left he said handing me his cloak you are marked with your longing   i turned my back on him   the road was covered in leaves & snow   you meet another & your longing fills her   you will meet another & kill her with your longing   i am full of this longing i thot   i meet another & i place my longing on her   i place my longing in my voice & say hello   hello she says   her voice is filled with longing   i place my longing in my eyes & see her   i see her thru my longing & she is filled with it   i see her thru my longing & my longing fills her   you will kill her with longing he said   you are empty from longing & you ask her to fill you   you ask her to fill you & she has nothing   i will kill her with my nothing i thot   i turned my back & walked down the road   he wrapped his cloak around me   she will not be there he said   the sky was a distant white   i watched his shadow grow smaller in the distance   i will kill her with this emptiness of longing   his shadow was blue & distant   i have killed her & she is no longer there i thot   i have killed myself with my longing   she is gone & i am no longer here   the white clouds drifted over him   i could kill with this longing emptiness   i wrapped his cloak around me   i wrapped his grey cloak around me & began to walk   the road curved beneath my feet   i met a boy digging in the earth   who are you i asked   he did not answer   who are you i asked   he wasnt there   i tried to imagine my window   i havent a name he said   i have no name tho i wish it   how far had i come   i do not know my name today   once was a day as once was another time my own life began a different course   there was no one   there was only the sea forever & ever as ever my own wish to leave it tho i swam free   oh what a day that was   i was the sea & the sea was in me   do you remember that day i stepped upon the shore   i do not know you   you have simply forgotten he said   the sun was large above the waves   you have forgotten because you do not wish to know   i do not know anymore   i have grown so tired of knowing   now i am full of longing & nothing fills me   now i am full of longing & nothing moves me   i lie on my bed longing   i lie on my bed & let my fingers move   oh heaven is there   surely heaven is there in that lifting   surely i could rise & enter that world knowing heaven was there   nothing is sure   as these things are they are only words one plays with to ones own ends   you are not longing she said   i looked up   you are longing for no one but yourself   the sky was blue   i put on my hat & began to walk   the day was grey   i have become nothing but my own emptiness & longing i thot    i met a boy digging in the sand    he had a sailors hat upon his head    why do you dig in the sand like that i asked    the grey cloak flapped about my knees    such a blue day    the roads wound around us    i did not know where i was that day    i had no name & he sat there playing in the sandy earth    i had no name & he would not tell me    the roads ran out from where we stood    he sat there playing    i had a name once he said    once i had a father & names made sense    once i had a mother to cherish that fathers naming    now nothing makes sense    now nothing has names    he gestured with his hand    i came from the sea he said yes he said yes i did come i did do that thing i came in from the sea    i came from the sea & now i sit here doing nothing    the roads ran away from the circle we stood in    i was lost in my feeling    i am full of longing i thot it seems i am full of memories    when you are lonely & without love you have nothing but memories of those you thot you loved    i have nothing but memories of you i thot    you say her face hung in the air    it didnt    you say her voice spoke in your ear    it didnt    dont you remember    you & the boy stood by the road    he was dressed in blue & a sailors hat    you looked towards the hills & thot about her    she was not there    you wore the cloak the stranger gave you    your fathers mark was on you & you hated him    you hated him & could not speak    the silence had driven you from her    dont you remember    it seems i can think of nothing else    i reached out to touch your breasts    your eyes were full of questions & fear    i ran my fingers over your nipples & you shivered    i ran my fingers over your belly as you touched my cock    i did not know you    i know no soft words to describe these things    i held you in my arms & kissed you    your mouth was full of bruising & longing    dont you remember    you had left the stranger far behind you    i dont know how far youd walked    the country changed from flat to hilly    the trees were larger &

the sky grew darker    you saw him in the distance he was just a young boy    the sailors hat sat back upon his head    hello you said    he did not answer    dont you remember    you started to cry & turned away    i asked you what was wrong    your eyes were filled with hurt & naming    i asked you what was wrong    you turned away    i said i was sorry was it something i'd done    your eyes looked past me    i placed a hand on your breast    you did not move    i placed a hand on your breast & pulled you to me your skin was damp & you trembled    my hand moved in your belly hair    you would not look at me    my hand touched your breast & stayed there    i moved my fingers in between your legs    you looked at me your eyes filled with hurt & naming    dont you recall    he said you did not know his name because you did not wish to remember    the trees grew in a circle there    the roads ran out from where you stood forever    you wanted to continue but it made no sense    you wanted to continue but her memory filled you    the memory filled you & you could not move    the boy asked what road youd come down you could not remember    the boy asked which road you would take    you did not know    the hole he'd dug was very deep    you looked past him into yourself    i dont remember    it was as if she stood next to me naked    i thot i heard her voice in my ear    i touched her breasts & belly & she shivered    god i was lonely    i longed to take her in my arms & love her    i looked in her eyes & ignored what i saw    i looked in her eyes & my eyes saw nothing    her mouth was so full of pain & hunger    my tongue touched her tongue & we said nothing    you didnt you say you touched her & you didnt    you say she shivered but the day was hot    you were sweating under your grey cloak    the boy removed his sailor hat & wiped his brow    there were just the two of you    it had been a long time since youd left the stranger    it mightve been a year or a day    the boy wiped his face & laughed    you really dont remember me do you he asked no you said & looked away i came from the sea i dont remember when you wouldnt look at him dont you remember god no god christ all i could feel was the loneliness i thot she was there i thot i touched her i never have words i never can tell you i touched her thighs & they parted i placed my cock between her legs & she shivered i could see the terror & chose not to god i was lonely i only wanted to hold her i only wanted to be in her ive never the words i speak of women & my tongue trembles i speak of women & my speech slurs there are no lovely words to praise them with ive only the cold words & cant speak god i am lonely for women i touch their breasts & shiver i touch their bodies & im damp with sweat i placed my cock between her legs & wept you didnt you say you wept but you didnt the boy asked you if you ever cried no you said i do he said sometimes he asked you why you never cried you would not answer are you ever happy he asked you would not answer sometimes im happy sometimes i wake up & gaze thru the window beyond my bed the sky is blue i feel joy inside me but i cant express it i feel joy & yet i am not joyous sometimes im joyous sometimes i wake up to blue skies full of joy & am joyous i put on my blue suit & sailor hat & go out you asked him where he lived he told you he lived by the side of the road a little further on you asked him which road he would not answer dont you remember no perhaps he was there i dont recall i thot i shoved my cock inside her i thot i thrust it in she moaned & shivered her whole body shuddered as i thrust it in i held her in my arms my cock thrust deep in her her body was damp & trembling our bellies stuck together god i get hungry for softness these words lack softness you used no words then you would not speak to him he spoke of the days he walked from his bed into the world he spoke of those days & his face lit with joy he was just a boy youd known him for a day or a week or two he spoke to you & you did not answer i was not aware of him she stood before me naked i shoved my cock in her i dont remember the boy you say he wore a sailor hat you say his suit was blue you say he dug a hole in the ground i dont remember the road was long youd been walking for months it seemed there was some house you were trying to get to the stranger had told you where to find it there was that night that one night before you met the boy my feet were sore i sat down on a rock to rest them a girl approached me from the woods her breasts were small & she trembled no there was no boy i remember she put a hand over her breasts & smiled no i dont remember youd been on the road for a long time before you met him it mightve been a month or a week since youd found the house the windows were shuttered you knocked & got no answer the door was barred you stood by the side of the road lost in your longing your fathers mark was on you & she was not there the house was empty & you screamed & shouted but she did not come she came she stepped out of the wood & smiled i read her eyes & ignored them god i was lonely i only wanted to hold her i only wanted to touch her skin i touch women & my hand trembles i kiss their bellies & am sick with sweat you are only lonely he said you lack love he said i looked into his eyes & knew it was true i looked into his eyes & knew my love was nothing i gave because i did not want to be given to i gave to hold my longing in by giving i denied my loneliness my loneliness denies my loving you are perfect in your loneliness he said you look in your mirrors full of self-love & loathing only you know your nothingness only you know your fear i looked into his eyes he seemed so young you are only a boy i said i said i know ive met you before you have never met me he said once he said once you knew me he touched his scarred nose the sailors hat sat back upon his head  you wear a grey cloak he said i knew a man once wore a grey cloak it was such a blue day  he poked his shovel in the dry earth & began to dig  no i said no i am not that man  i met him once i said  the man i knew wore a grey cloak like you he said  i turned away & began to walk  his voice was very distant  i turned & looked back at the spot where he had been  i drew the grey cloak around my shoulders & began to walk i was cold & trembling  the moon rose over the trees  i am sick of this i thot  i meet people but it is all for nothing  i meet people & say goodbye knowing nothing  i lay down the cloak wrapped tight around me  the trees formed a circle where i lay asleep  he raised his head & looked at me  who are you he asked i do not know who you are  i am named i said  can you not see the mark  yes you are marked he said  i felt the sweat form on my body i let the grey cloak fall open  who understands this i thot  i met a woman once who understood me she reached out her hand & touched me  the longing was gone  i was no longer full of the longing when she touched me  no one understands what is least of all myself  i do not understand  i looked up thru the trees at the moon  i do not understand what has made me most myself i thot  this selfs as known as these words i write if less familiar  oh it is not for nothing  no it is not all pain  sometimes the day opens & i flower  sometimes the day opens & i move with freedom thru the tall blue of it  all these words are only nothing  all these words are only sounds  i dance with the sounds  i sing with the sounds  the sound is all the meaning that there is  the sound is the loving  the sound is the longing  oh god i am so full of sound  i open my mouth & sound escapes  i open my mouth to let the sound escape  my body fills with it  i vibrate with the sound  i hate the words  the words destroy the sounds with useless meanings  the meanings pile up & the sound is lost  i scream with the sound  i live in the sound  the sound flows around me i am lost in it  oh surely this is knowing to live & breathe & celebrate the sound  all heaven is sound  i am caught in the sound  father you named me but gave me no sound  it was a flat lifeless thing this naming  now i dream i walk by the sea & the sea is sound the waves wash over me & the waves are sound  oh these words are useless  i swim in the sound & the sound surrounds me  i swallow the sound  i scream the sound  the sound is me & the sound surrounds  ah i remember  christ i remember  i lie here in this circle of trees my heart heavy with remembering  in the sound my heart is light  in the midst of the sound the hope is endless  i was a just a young boy  i remember it well  i sat where the roads came together in a circle beyond the great woods  i sat digging holes in the earth listening to the sound  a man approached me from the long roads  he wore a grey cloak & his eyes were troubled  i spoke to him but he did not hear me  i spoke to him but he looked away  i remember the sun was shining  hello i said  he did not answer  the air was still around him  i remember i listened but he made no sound  who are you i asked i do not know you  the sky was blue & i lay back in the tall green grass watching him  he spoke of nothing but his eyes screamed  such perfect loneliness i thot  i thot he has surrounded himself with loneliness & now he walks thru the world encased in that hunger he cannot escape from  i grabbed his grey cloak & tugged at it  who are you i shouted  he made no answer  the clouds floated white above us  far away i saw the line of trees  who are you i shouted tugging at his cloak  his eyes were troubled & locked in their loneliness  who are you i shouted hitting him with my shovel  the shovel banged uselessly against his chest  he walked past me where i sat digging in the earth  hello i said  he did not turn around  hello i said would you like to rest here  i watched him disappearing in the distance towards the wood    i lay back in the grass & watched the clouds blow over    oh i remember christ i remember    jesus how could i ever forget    i live with the fucking thing    i carry the fucking memories like a wound across my throat    jesus i'll never forget the fucker    he stood there with his blank eyes looking thru me    fuck off i shouted    i smashed the shovel against his face    i watched the wound grow where his nose had been    cocksucking motherfucker just get the fuck out of here    i screamed & kicked at him    fuck off fuck off    he held his hands up to catch the blood & backed away cocksucker i screamed dirty fucking cocksucker get away from me    i dont want your fucking nothingness    get away motherfucker    get away the ground was spotted with blood    god i remember    christ i can never forget    he ran screaming down the road    i remember the sound possessed him his body shook as he ran & he held his face with his hands    i remember the gaping hole below his eyes where i'd smashed his nose in    get away motherfucker get away    i buried my face in the grass & sobbed    i remember the wind was high    i stood up quietly    i couldnt see him anymore    i took the earth & rubbed it over my face    i took the earth in my hands & ate it    i let my tongue lick the hole i'd dug    i licked the shovel clean with my tongue    oh i remember    christ i remember    are you happy i whispered    nothing answered    are you happy in your loneliness    oh i get hungry for sound    i brush my fingers over the soft flesh of her body & feel the sound thats in her    oh to be in that sound    in the heart of the sound there is peace    in the heat of the sound there is happiness    christ i get lonely in this stillness    i sit here at this desk surrounded by the stillness & death of this city    the streets seem so empty of sound    he stood up    the trees grew close around him    another calls my name & i rise somewhere someone writes my history & i am named    i hate you for that naming    i hate what you do    i am left with no place to run to no place to rest its useless if only you stopped writing i could sit down & think but you did do it yes i did do it yes i did smash his face in the stupid cocksucker was asking for it i was only ten you know oh i mightve been younger i sat in the sand digging as he approached hello i said hello its a lovely day i remember he said nothing i remember the air was still around him oh i was hungry for sound all i wanted was one hello all i wanted was that one sound he said nothing the longing sprang up in my throat & choked me yes i remember oh god i remember i carry the longing for that sound everywhere i carry the longing for that sound & grow weak yes i am lonely i am i reach out but my hands stay still i reach out & smile indifferently hello i say hello how are you no one answers i close the sounds down around me & draw inside i close the sounds down & make the longing me ah it is all so perfect yes it is a perfect thing i carry the longing but the longings me i put the longing inside me & say nothing people say hello & i do not answer hello they say hello how are you the stillness is perfect the silence is a perfect thing no sound comes to disturb it their lips move but i do not hear them their lips move but my lips are still it could all be so perfect it could all be such a perfect perfect thing once was a day remember that day that one day i knew the silence didnt work hello she said & my lips trembled hello she said & the silence broke he looked at her frightened who are you he asked who are you i did not know you were here you came so suddenly thru the trees there no she said no hello he said she looked at him strangely i have been walking a long time he said looking at her long hair her red dress i lay down in this wood & fell asleep your face she said your face you have cut yourself no no it is nothing she ran her fingers over the crushed bones of his nose i am named i said i carry the mark wherever i go wherever i go the mark is on me what is this naming she asked who does this i looked in her eyes & remembered i looked in her eyes & saw myself there it had all been so perfect it had all been such a perfect perfect thing christ but the silence had been perfect now i was filled with names now i was numb with naming i am no longer perfect i said she looked at me strangely i said to her i said i am no longer perfect cant you see it dont you know it you do know it dont you you know i am no longer perfect i have broken that perfect silence i said she smiled & said nothing i was perfect in my silence i thot god but i was perfect till you came he looked at her strangely yes i know you she said i have seen you so many times what do you know he said i know your silences she said i took his hand touch me i said he trembled touch my breasts i said he did not touch them take my nipples between your teeth i said he let his fingers graze my belly hair i held them there he let his fingers enter me i don't know your name i said she smiled i let my lips graze her belly hair she held them there oh how i longed for the silences you are screaming i said you say nothing but your screaming i pressed my face between her thighs kiss me there i said he kissed me i felt his tongue in my cunt kiss me there i said he kissed me god how i kissed her she held my cock in her hands come inside me she said guiding me in god i remember christ i remember oh that was the day that was the day this perfection ended it had been so long so very very long of course i remember i do remember there is no doubt i remember yes i know you she said he took the grey cloak & wrapped it round her my hand was on his cock he looked so frightened i love you i said guiding him inside me i said i love you and held him inside me he was so much loneliness he was so much distance i looked thru his eyes into the sky my breasts were full of him   my belly sang with him   i love you i said i love you   he looked past me into the grass   i said i do love you & held him to me   he came inside me   he came & filled me with his loneliness   his loneliness filled me & i lay back weeping   i love you i said   he filled me with his loneliness & naming   i know you i said   once was a time i knew you   once was a time i stood in the door of my house   you came along the road & saw me   hello you said   i said nothing   you said something again   i said what i said   you entered in   i looked past you towards the mountains & the sea   you led me back inside & we made love   oh i remember   i surely do remember

now i carry you with me wherever i go   now wherever i go i feel you inside me   i love you i said   his nose was broken   i do love you i did say   i did say that you know   he didnt hear me   he lay on top of me filling me with his breathing   i love you   i ran my fingers down his back & kissed him   i do love you   i lay on my back in the grass watching the clouds blow past   he lay on top of me his cock inside me   i do remember that day   as it is these are only dreams i have foretold the wish of to be made whole as it was that day he lay inside me dreaming   he lay his loneliness inside me & dreamed   do you remember it as it was   i remember it   do you know i cried   i know you cried   he lay on top of me dreaming   he looked so frightened   you have hurt yourself i said touching his broken face   no it is nothing he said   i lay there wishing his cock inside me   you are lost in your loneliness i said   he lay on top of me his cock inside me   you are lost in your lovelessness   i hold you in me but you feel nothing   god he seemed hungry   christ he seemed hungry in his silence   i took off his sailor hat   i love you i said   i took off his grey cloak & his name   i do love you i said   he lay on top of me his cock inside me   i do love you   i wiped his fingers   i wiped the blood from his face   yes i love you i said   he lay inside me

i love you i do love you i said   he lay inside me my

cock inside me i do love we i said we lay inside me our cock inside me we do love we we said yes we do love we we watched the clouds blow over we lay inside us lonely we touched our broken face we picked up our tiny shovel we licked it clean we placed our face between our thighs we love us we said lonely we love us such a blue day the road stretched out forever from the window where we lay sleeping

3

i have said everything i can say having started out so sure i know there are times when words make sense times when all this talking seems necessary it doesnt now    sometimes i go back there to the street where i lived the spot where the dance hall stood back to the room i lay in thru my sickness the place i found the roads spread out from sit & scratch at the earth with my shovel my pen & try to start again that way    it doesnt work    long ago i saw that long ago i knew that that was no good    now i know im thru with her

for good there is no point in continuing this story
so much seems like coincidence like some novel
you dream up in a bad year goodbye mother
goodbye father goodbye lonely feeling its be-
coming vital now that we all quit this now its be-
coming vital that we all stop i must speak to you
without her presence i need to tell you things she
wouldnt want me to say maybe i wont be there
when you put this book down someone will be
there its all so simple really its all so straightahead
it cant end like it always does once i asked them
all to speak to me all of them now im asking you ive
always felt too shy i never thot youd listen i still
wonder if you'll listen to me at some point you just
have to put the fear aside at some point we just
have to talk when you read this i want it to be me
when you read this i want to be there its so easy to
beome maudlin its so easy to be insincere every-
thing is here as it happened i want to be sure youre
here saying hello to me i cant be sure its unfair
really to ask that of you when you put this book
down i wont be there someone will be there its so
simple isnt it all one has to do is speak honestly
all you have to do is say what you feel to speak to
anyone is so simple to speak to anyone you just put
your book down look them in the eye & tell them what
it is exactly that youre feeling

## Two Words: A Wedding

*for Rob & Sheron*

There are things you have words for, things you do not have words for. There are words that encompass all your feelings & words that encompass none. There are feelings you have that are like things to you, picked up & placed in the pocket, worn like the cloth the pocket is attached to, like a skin you live inside of. There is a body of feeling, of language, of friends; the body politic, the body we are carried inside of till birth, the body we carry our self inside of till death, a body of knowledge that tells of an afterlife, a heaven, an unknown everything we have many words for but cannot encompass. There are relationships between words & concepts, between things, between life & death, between friends & family, between each other & some other other. We wed words to things, people to feelings, speak of a true wedding of the mind & heart, intuition & intellect, & out of this form our realities. Our realities are wedded one to another, concepts & people are joined, new people conceived within that mesh of flesh & realities, are carried forward in the body of the mother, the family, the bodily love we have for one another. They are creating their own reality each step of the way, daily, another kind of reality is born, each new word, person, expanding our vocabulary, our concepts, new realities are conceived, our old reality changes, the 'real' grows realer every day. We are marrying the flesh to the flesh, the word to the daily flux of lives we know & don't know, our friends grow older & marry, raise children as you once were children with mothers & fathers of your own, grow older, so many things you still lack words for, struggle to wed the inner & outer worlds, the self to some other self or selves, confess your love & struggle with one another, together, conscious there is this word in you, your name, & that you are yet another thing or things you will never encompass, never exhaust the possibilities of, because you are wedded to the flux of life, because we are words and our meanings change.

1978

## Still

From the banks of the river, the spray from the rapids making the grass & clay slippery, thru the dark shadows beneath the oaks, the ground worn bare in spots, packed hard from the comings & goings of unnumbered feet, an old footpath makes its way to the edge of the lawn. From the mouth of the river where it loses itself in the larger waters, where the rock & debris strewn shore is daily washed by the movement of the waves, another path winds its way up the bluff face, turns left along the top of the bluff, right along the banks of the river, joining the older footpath as it nears the wood or, if the other direction is taken, losing itself miles later in the long grass that overlooks the vast body of the sea. To walk that way, to look first to the right towards the distant horizon of sea & sky, then left towards the house, makes the house appear as it really is: a small two-storey building to which a front verandah & a back balcony have been added; a farmhouse whose barn has long since disappeared; a house built for a different time & thus a different purpose & place. From the bluffs in a direct line with the little orchard another path winds its way towards the house, bypasses it to loop thru the orchard & then, almost as if continuing the back sidewalk, turns to the right & runs straight out towards the middle of the mountain range. Nearing the beginning of the foothills the path winds & twists, making its way thru ravines & gulleys, old river beds, finding its way to the valleys that run into the heart of the mountains. From those same mountains numerous trails snake out & join to make two main ones: the one that finds its way eventually into the orchard & a second one that follows the course of the river, joining, finally, the older path that runs towards the house thru the oak wood. The path to the orchard takes three days by foot, & the one that follows the twists & curves of the river six days, sections of the trail continually being obliterated by collapsing river banks until, finally, as the wheat field is reached, the edges of that more precisely defined area can be followed straight across towards the lawn on the left side of the house, the long grass & wheat making passage easy even tho no path exists. From the edge of the lawn, from the point where the old footpath ends, the white pebbled surface of the winding path that leads to the front door begins. In spring & summer the flowers blooming in the large & small flowerbeds flood the air round the walk with perfume, & the distance from the edge of the lawn to the front verandah is marked by a shifting & blending of fragrance & colour. It is this path & the path from the sea that are favoured in these seasons. Returning from the beach in late July thru the long grass at the bluff's edge, or emerging from the dark wood into the bright sun of the lawn, seeing the house, the house appears larger, more imposing, & the curtained windows seem inviting, mysterious, holding forth a promise that is never articulated. In fall the trails to & from the mountains are more frequented, the mud room providing an area in which to remove boots & coats, a place to deposit the sprays of dying leaves, the bits of fossils. As these routes are travelled, the house disappears then reappears as the path dips, turns, moves in behind the hills & rock outcroppings, out again, up, the roof now visible, then the whole building growing larger or smaller depending on the direction travelled. In winter all this is altered, the paths curving around the house & across the lawn from various directions to reach the back door, the front door ignored again until spring. But in the other three seasons of the year unmarked continuations of all these paths, of other paths only temporarily established, criss-cross the lawn toward the front verandah, all of them joining at the foot of the verandah stairs. The coco-matting that covers the stairs is worn &, in places, the staples have worked loose, causing the matting to slide dangerously. The strips covering the porch are worn too & the legs of the couch whose back faces the front railing of the verandah, whose cloth surface is also worn from years of use, first in the livingroom of the house & now, for years, on the front verandah, have worn thru the matting completely & rest on the grey painted floorboards. Only the swinging seat appears new because of the coat of white paint that has been given to it sometime in the past year, sometime in the spring so that the winter snow & frozen air have had no change yet to chip & crack the surface. But the easy chair & the couch, part of the same set purchased when the house was newer, are comfortable & inviting, make sitting on the porch in the warm summer evenings more pleasurable, & the hanging baskets & stone vases give the porch a garden air that the surrounding flower beds accent. Seen from the foot of the verandah stairs, surrounded as they are by the scent of flowers & the distant murmuring of the river, the front door seems less inviting or, more exactly, a thing to be postponed, something to keep closed, sealed, until the moment it is absolutely necessary to use it. As fall turns to winter & the wind from the sea blows in flat across the bluffs, the door is something longed for on returning from skating on the cold ice of the river, longed for precisely because it must remain sealed & the path around the house to the back door seems infinitely long & difficult of access. Running up the path from the river thru the falling rain, reaching the porch, the porch is something to linger on while watching the lightning dance across the sky & strike the distant ground, the front lawn at least three times, the lightning rod on the peak of the house once, & the front door, closed or open, is a source of security, the knowledge that it exists, can be opened, that the house is there & can be entered, reassuring, a presence that embraces by its very familiarity, its nearness &, in reaching for the brass doorknob, turning it, opening the door, a ritual is reenacted whose meaning deepens with each passing year. Pulling the screen door open to turn the handle of the inner door or, the inner door already open or, the screen door not yet in place or already removed & only the one door then to open, crossing the threshold as the door swings inward &, entering the ground floor hallway, turning back to watch the lightning or to close the door quickly because it is winter, because it should not have been opened in the first place no vestibule to absorb the chill air, or leaving it open because the screen is in place & the house is still hot from the day's accumulations &, standing in the front hallway as the screen door or the front door swings shut, one enters finally, or for the first time, the inside of the house. In the diningroom to the left the table has been set. Viewed thru the french doors the place settings appear, momentarily, as if painted onto the surface of the oak table, the precise arrangement of the blue cloth napkins, blue china plates, silver cutlery to either side, & the blue candles in the cut glass candlestick holders (removed from the mantle & placed in the centre of the table) forming, with the cut glass bowl of white chrysanthemums, a perfect still life. Thru the leaded windows the back of the easy chair is visible, the couch, the white pebbled path winding off between the flowerbeds towards the river. The armchair that had sat in front of the window has been placed in front of one of the place settings & a number of other diningroom chairs have been moved from places against the wall & arranged around the table. The window that looks out on the wheatfield is open & a sliding screen has been placed in it to both hold it open & keep any straying insects out. From the fireplace, thru the french doors in the opposite wall, the front door is visible, the clothes rack, the umbrella stand, the french doors across the hall &, from the one doorway into the other a continuing view of the front lawn is seen thru each succeeding window, each frame (those in the diningroom, the leaded ones in the livingroom, the open doorway of the house in between) recapitulating part of the earlier scene while adding fresh elements to it. In this way the beginning of the woods is first glimpsed from the diningroom (a few trees on the left side of the frame), dominates the whole of the open doorway & then continues to dominate the landscape as seen from the livingroom. A number of magazines lie scattered on the couch to the right as that room is entered: recent numbers of technical journals devoted to particular issues in physics & philosophy, a poetry magazine, a copy of a national gossip monthly & copies of various international news weeklies. The books that were on top of the ladder at the far end of the room have been put away & a number of new volumes have been removed from the shelves & stacked on the floor as if the system by which the books had been arranged is now being reorganized. More volumes are stacked by the easy chairs in front of the fireplace. Along the hall from the front door toward the kitchen nothing has changed. Each painting retains its location, the frames dusted but the arrangement undisturbed, & the letter on the little mail table under the mirror remains unopened & has been joined by a second one. As the door to the kitchen is pushed open, the hinges squeaking as the door swings inward, the hum of the fridge is audible in the hall until the door swings shut again. Here the counter shows signs of food preparation: flour sprinkled on the red top; a cutting board on which a knife rests exactly in the middle of a scattering of small cubes of diced green pepper; a bowl to the right of them containing lettuce, tomatoes, & shredded strips of carrots; in the sink, a number of pots, only their handles visible above the white mound of suds. The preparation table has the largest of the five cutting boards lying in the middle of it & in the middle of the cutting board a roasting chicken has been placed awaiting the toasting of the bread for the stuffing. The chairs around the red table have been pulled back as if in haste & the door to the mud room & the door to the basement are both lying open. From the top of the cellar stairs the basement is too dark to allow any details to be visible & neither the light switch there nor the light switch at the foot of the stairs to the second floor is working. As each of the carpeted steps is climbed, the view that is possible thru the window at the top changes so that first only the sky is visible & then the edge of the bluffs, more & more lawn &, finally, the top stair being reached & the landing stepped onto, the sea beyond all of them. One of the dolls has been removed from the small bedroom & placed in the white wooden chair to the left of the window. The curtains in the small bedroom are drawn, the covers of the bed thrown back, & one of the pillows has fallen off the bed onto the floor & is blocking the door to the closet. The new dolls have been added to the shelves on the right side of the window & the books on the shelves to the left have been rearranged in alphabetical order & stood upright, shiny new blue bookends holding them in place. The mirror in the dresser is tilted so that the back of the top edge is pressing against the wall behind it & the hairline cracks in the painted blue plaster ceiling are reflected. The red carpet in the hall clashes slightly with the blue in the bedroom, more because of the intensity of the pattern than the colour, & here & there has begun to wear thin. In the front bedroom on the left side of the house a suitcase has been thrown on the bed, the contents already taken out & hung behind the closed door of the closet. A dictionary has been borrowed from the bedroom across the hall & placed on the small writing table along with a portable typewriter whose case rests on the floor beside the chair. The window at the front of the house has been thrown open & the fragrances from the various flowerbeds have begun to fill the room & to move thru the open doorway into the hall. The second bedroom is empty. The door to the closet lies open & inside it a number of boxes have been stored, some labelled 'books,' others labelled 'winter clothes,' 'knickknacks,' as if someone were moving or had moved, the process of packing or unpacking not yet finished & the boxes placed here until they could be dealt with. The curtains in the room have been drawn & the light filtering thru them gives the room a quiet, forlorn feeling which the faint perfume of the flowers only intensifies. Across the hall the door to the large bedroom lies open, the window facing it looking out over the bluffs & sea, & in the distance, almost at the very horizon, storm clouds are forming, lightning crackling & dancing on the surface of the distant waves, tho on the lawn around the house the sun is still shining & the breeze has not yet shifted in intensity or direction. The cover on the sewing machine in front of the window has been replaced, even tho the basket which has been brought into the room, & now sits to the left of the sewing machine table, contains a number of torn pieces of clothing, & a package of small white buttons has been placed on the right side of the table. A file folder lies open on the desk to the right of the hallway door, the folder's exposed top sheet appearing to be part of a journal or novel, difficult to determine exactly from such a small fragment, to which a number of revisions have been made, the different dates of the revisions hinted at by the shifting colours & shades of ink. A dictionary lies open on the desk to the left of the folder tho the significance of the pages revealed is not immediately apparent since none of the words defined on those particular pages of the dictionary are written on the exposed page of the folder. There are a number of pens lying to the right of the file folder & a small message pad, devoid of writing, in the surface of which the indecipherable indentations made in the course of writing many now non-existent notes appear. Here too the bed is unmade, the pillows having fallen on the floor & a book, a mystery novel, lies open face down on the rumpled sheets. The closet door is open & a number of items of clothing have fallen on the closet floor. The closet light has also been left on. From the hall window at the front the rapids in the river are clearly visible, the white foam of the water as it smashes against the rocks creating tiny whirlpools, easily seen beyond the leafy green branches of the oaks. Down the hall thru the open door of the bathroom, the clothes hamper is visible to the right of the door, is empty when the top is lifted, when the threshold is crossed the top of the clothes hamper is lifted up, placed on the floor, & some article of clothing is or is not dropped into the open basket. The window in the wall opposite the door looks out on the mountains, & the bathtub, wet from recent use, appears as white & cold as the distant peaks. The bathmat is wet & water has pooled on the tiles near the tub & sink. Bits of hair have been caught in both drains & if either set of taps is turned on there is a long wait before hot water comes. The towels which had hung on the wall to the right of the window are now lying in a clump on the flour between the toilet & the end wall. The weights on the scale have been moved, pulling the balancing mechanism down because of the lack of a counter-balance. In the hall the red carpet just outside the door of the bathroom is damp & a number of darker damp spots appear in a semicircle around the larger wet area. Along the hall the door to the upper balcony lies open, the balustrade visible thru the screen door, the orchard beyond, the mountains over which the storm clouds that only a short time ago seemed a safe distance out at sea are now massing. On the inside wall just to the right of the balcony door is the switch which controls the frosted light fixture in the ceiling of the porch and, at night, because of the bug lamp inside it, it casts a muted yellow light. From the hallway of the house looking out onto the balcony a table is visible on the right, two wicker chairs, an ashtray & a deck of cards on the table top &, to the left, thru the thick mesh of the screen door, the porch light not yet on tho the sky is darkening as the storm clouds begin to move closer to the house & the sun to set behind the distant peaks, in the quickening dusk we are aware of two other chairs, another table, & two people who suddenly begin talking.

## The Vagina

1 I never had one.

2 I lived inside a woman for nine months & inside this male shell all of my life. I floated around on that side of the wall poking & kicking her not looking for exits till I needed them. There came a time I needed you vagina to get thru into this world. First thing I say at the light of day is 'waaah,' Ma.

3 I thot they all were hairless even tho I bathed with my mother I thot they all were like the little girl's who came naked to the door I delivered the paper to when I was nine even tho I read the typed porno stories my brother brought back from the navy when I was ten I thot they all were hairless like the nude women's in the sunbathing magazines in the pool hall in Port Arthur even tho I had to know different somewhere I thot they all were hairless & they weren't.

4 I always wanted one. I grew up wanting one. I thot cocks were okay but vaginas were really nifty. I liked that name for them because it began with 'v' and went 'g' in the middle. I never heard my mother or my sister mention them by name. They were an unspoken mouth & that was the mouth where real things were born. So I came out of that mouth with my mouth flapping 'waaah.' Oh I said that. I said that. I said 'waaah' Ma again & again after I was born.

5 When I was eleven this kid I knew took me to the drugstore where he worked & showed me some sanitary napkins for men. He said, 'you wear these when you get your period.' I remember he pointed the box out to me & it was way up in the back of this unlit top shelf. I figured I must have some kind of vestigial vagina which was bound to open. I waited almost two years. I never had one.

6 When sex happened I realized it was all a matter of muscles. I liked the way her muscles worked. She liked the way my muscle worked. It wasn't the one thing or the other thing but the way the two of them worked together. And that was where all the power & the feelings sprang from – the muscles. Alive alive oh.

7 Doorway. Frame. Mouth. Opening. Passage. The trick is to get from there to here thru her. Or the way Ellie misread that sign on the highway for years: RIGHT LANE MUST EXIST. And of course it's the old conundrum – the exit's the entrance. Exit Ma & I exist. And when I fell in love with Ellie I was entranced. Into a world. The world. This world. Our world. Worlds.

## The Mouth

1 You were never supposed to talk when it was full. It was better to keep it shut if you had nothing to say. You were never supposed to shoot it off. It was better to be seen than heard. It got washed out with soap if you talked dirty. You were never supposed to mouth-off, give them any of your lip, turn up your nose at them, give them a dirty look, an evil eye or a baleful stare. So your mouth just sat there, in the middle of your still face, one more set of muscles trying not to give too much away. 'Hey! SMILE! what's the matter with you anyway?'

2 Probably there are all sorts of stories. Probably my mouth figures in all sorts of stories when I was little but I don't remember any of them. I don't remember any stories about my mouth but I remember it was there. I remember it was there and I talked & sang & ate & used it all the time. I don't remember anything about it but the mouth remembers. The mouth remembers what the brain can't quite wrap its tongue around & that's what my life's become. My life's become my mouth's remembering, telling stories with the brain's tongue.

3 I must have been nine. I'm pretty sure I was nine because I remember I was the new boy in school. I remember I was walking on my way there, the back way, thru the woods, & here was this kid walking towards me, George was his name, & I said 'hi George' & he said 'I don't like your mouth' & grabbed me & smashed my face into his knee. It was my first encounter with body art or it was my first encounter with someone else's idea of cosmetic surgery. It was translation or composition. He rearranged me.

4 The first dentist called me the Cavity Kid & put 35 fillings into me. The second dentist said the first dentist was a charlatan, that all the fillings had fallen out, & put 38 more fillings in me. The third dentist had the shakes from his years in the prisoner of war camp & called me his 'juicy one,' saliva frothing from my mouth as his shakey hand approached me. The fourth dentist never looked at me. His nurse put me out with the sleeping gas & then he'd enter the room & fill me. The fifth dentist said my teeth were okay but my gums would have to go, he'd have to cut me. The sixth dentist said well he figured an

operation on the foot was okay coz the foot was a long way away but the mouth was just a little close to where he thot he lived & boy did we ever agree because I'd begun to see that every time I thot of dentists I ended the sentence with the word 'me.' My mouth was me. I wasn't any ancient Egyptian who believed his Ka was in his nose – nosiree – I was just a Kanadian kid & had my heart in my mouth every time a dentist approached me.

5 It all begins with the mouth. I shouted waaa when I was born, maaa when I could name her, took her nipple in, the rubber nipple of the bottle later, the silver spoon, mashed peas, dirt, ants, anything with flavour I could shove there, took the tongue & flung it 'round the mouth making sounds, words, sentences, tried to say the things that made it possible to reach him, kiss her, get my tongue from my mouth into some other. I liked that, liked the fact the tongue could move in mouths other than its own, & that so many things began there – words did, meals, sex – & tho later you travelled down the body, below the belt, up there you could belt out a duet, share a belt of whiskey, undo your belts & put your mouths together. And I like the fact that we are rhymed, mouth to mouth, & that it begins here, on the tongue, in the pun, comes from mouth her mouth where we all come from.

6 I always said I was part of the oral tradition. I always said poetry was an oral art. When I went into therapy my therapist always said I had an oral personality. I got fixated on oral sex, oral gratification & notating the oral reality of the poem. At the age of five when Al Watts Jr was still my friend I actually said, when asked who could do something or other, 'me or Al' & only years later realized how the truth's flung out of you at certain points & runs on ahead. And here I've been for years running after me, trying to catch up, shouting 'it's the oral,' 'it all depends on the oral,' everybody looking at my bibliography, the too many books & pamphlets, saying with painful accuracy: 'that bp – he really runs off at the mouth.'

## The Tonsils

1 They said 'you don't need them' but they were keen to cut them out. They said 'if they swell up they'll choke you to death' so you learned they cut things off if they might swell up. There were two of them in their sacs & they hung there in your throat. They cut them off.

2 I didn't have them long enough to grow attached to them but they were attached to me. It was my first real lesson in having no choice. It was my only time ever in a hospital as a kid & I wasn't even sick. I wasn't even sick but I had the operation. I had the operation that I didn't want & I didn't say 'no' because there was no choice really. I had everybody who was bigger than me telling me this thing was going to happen & me crying a lot & them telling me it was good for me. It was my first real lesson in having no attachments.

3 Almost everyone I knew had their tonsils out. Almost everyone I knew was told 'it's good for you.' Even tho none of us who had our tonsils out ever knew any kid who choked to death from having them in, almost everyone we knew had their tonsils out.

4 I miss my tonsils. I think my throat used to feel fuller. Now my throat feels empty a lot & maybe that's why I eat too fast filling the throat with as much as I can. Except food is no substitute for tonsils. The throat just gets empty again.

5 I was told I didn't need my tonsils. Maybe this is the way it is. Maybe as you grow older they tell you there are other bits you don't need & they cut them out. Maybe they just like cutting them out. Maybe tonsils are a delicacy doctors eat & the younger they are the sweeter. Maybe this is just paranoia. I bet if I had a lobotomy they could cut this paranoia out.

6 What cutting remarks! What rapier wit! What telling thrusts! Ah cut it out! Cut it short! He can't cut it! You said a mouthful!

7 There are two of them & they hang there in your throat. There are two of them in sacs & they swell up. Now there are none. Gosh these words seem empty!

## The Lungs: A Draft

*for Robert Kroetsch*

1 This is a breath line. I said. This is a breathline. Line up, he said. Suck your stomach in Nichol, I don't want to see you breathe. I didn't breathe. This was a no breath line. He said. Six or eight or ten of us not breathing while he walked down the line, holding our breath while he looked us over, while he chose one of us to punch in the gut, to see how tough our stomach muscles were he said, stomachs pulled in, lungs pushed out, waiting while he paced back and forth, while he paused in front of each of us and then moved on, this small smile playing across his lips. Waiting. A breathless line. I said.

2 I was staying at Bob and Smaro's place in Winnipeg. I was sleeping on the floor in Smaro's study. I was getting up early in the morning, like I tend to do, getting up early and going into the livingroom. I was sitting down in a chair and reading a copy of a new book on literary theory or literary criticism Smaro had brought back from some recent trip as she tends to do. I was just turning the page, just beginning to get into the book when Bob appeared at the top of the stairs, when Bob came down the stairs from the upper floor, not really awake, came down the stairs anyway, Bob, muttering to himself, 'life, the great tyrant that makes you go on breathing.' And I thought about breathing. I thought about life. I thought about those great tyrants the lungs, about the lung poems I've tried to perfect in various ways, the lung poems Bob's written, written about, lung forms. And I thought about the lungs sitting there, inside the chest – inhaling – exhaling. And I thought to myself, to myself because Bob was in no mood to hear it, I thought 'life's about going the lung distance.' Just that. And it is.

3 We were maybe five, Al Watts Jr and me, no more than five, and we had snuck out back, behind the garage, to try a smoke. It was just the way you read it in all those nostalgic memoirs of male childhood. It was authentic. It was a prairie day in Winnipeg in the late 40s and there we were, two buddies sharing a furtive puff on a stolen cigarette. And just like in all the other stories the father showed up, Al Watts Sr, suddenly appeared around the corner of the garage and said 'so you boys want to smoke, eh?' If only we'd read the stories. If only

we'd had the stories read to us. We'd have known then how the whole thing had to end, we'd have known what part the dad plays in these kinds of tales. But we hadn't. We didn't. We said yes we really did want to smoke. And we did. Al Watts Sr took us home, took us back to his study, the room he very seldom took us into, and opened up his box of cigars and offered one to each of us. We should have known. We really should have known when he lit them for us and told us to really suck in, to take that smoke right down into our lungs, we should have known what was coming. We didn't. We did it just the way he said. We sucked that smoke right in, right down to our lungs, and of course we started hacking, of course we started coughing, trying to fling the cigars away. But he made us take another smoke, he made us take another three or four good drags on the cigar, until our bodies were racked from the coughing, until our lungs ached from the lunge and heave of trying to push the smoke out. And we didn't want to smoke anymore, I didn't want to smoke anymore, I never really wanted to touch a cigarette again. Even when I was a teenager and hanging out with Easter Egg on his old scow down in Coal Harbour and he'd offer me a toke, I never could take the smoke into my lungs again. Except that after I turned 30 I started smoking cigars. And even though I didn't take the smoke into my lungs, even though I just held it there in the mouth and let it go, when I thought about it it really didn't make much sense. It didn't you know. Look what had happened to me with Al Watts Sr and Al Watts Jr those many many years ago. This wasn't supposed to be the outcome. This wasn't supposed to be the way the story goes. But it was as if the lungs wanted me to do it. As if the lungs had a memory all their own and I was forced to relive it. Not a primal scream but a primal puff, primal smoke from a primal prairie fire. As if the whole childhood episode had been like one of those moral tales where the reader takes a different lesson from the one the writer intended. Or like one of those shaggy dog jokes, where the punch line comes way after the joke should have ended, way after the person listening has lost all interest in what's being said. Lung time. Different from the head's.

4 When do you first think of your lungs? When you're young and tiny and turning blue and you can't get your breath because something is happening to you like my mom told me it happened to me? When you're five and choking over your first smoke like I just told you?

When you start to sing in the choir and the choirmaster tells you to really fill your lungs with air, your stomach, and support the sound from down there, inside the body? When you take up running, gasp for that last breath hoping to bring the tape nearer, the finish line, hoping the lungs will hold for the final lunge? Do you think of them then? In a moment like this, trying to remember, can you even say 'I remember this about my lungs'? No. No. Almost no memories at all. Only the notion that they're there pumping away, just beneath the surface of these lines, however much these lines do or don't acknowledge them. One of those parts you can't do without. Two of them. 'The bellows,' he bellows, airing his opinion. Because to air is human. To forgive the divine. Bellowing our prays, our songs. Bellowing our lung-ings.

5 A draft he calls it. Like it blew in through a crack in the mind. Just a bunch of hot air. As when you're really hot, get the cadences to fall, the syllables to trot past the eye and ear just the way you see and hear them in the mind. As tho the mind tapped the lung and each thot hung there in its proper place. 'It's just a draft. I'll get it right later.' He feels the breath heave. He hears the words start as the heart pumps and the lungs take all that air and squeeze it in there, into the blood stream flows thru the mind. No next time when the lungs stop. Like that last sentence on the tongue, hangs in the air after the lungs have pressed their last square inch of it out in the absolute moment of death, only the body left: 'I'll get it right next time.'

## Sum of the Parts

1 So many things inside me I am not in touch with. So many things I depend on that I never see, pray I never see. As in the horror movie when the monster's taloned hand reaches in and pulls out your living spleen. So many things with such strange names. The sound of them is enough to make me vomit. And when I do, well, there it is, something from inside me, and I am in touch with it, can smell it, taste it, feel it, praying I'll never have to again, praying it will stop, the contraction in the throat, the sound from beyond the tongue, more in touch with my insides than I really wanted.

2 If you're unlucky you get to meet them. If you're lucky you never get to meet them at all, they just nestle there, inside your body, monitoring, processing, producing, while you go about your life, oblivious. And this is the real organ music, the harmony of these spheres, the way the different organs play together, work, at that level beyond consciousness of which all consciousness is composed, the real unconscious, the unseen.

3 It's the old problem of writing about something you know nothing about. I can do the research, read the books, but it's not the same. It's not the same. Tho they name the organs and the names are the same they're not the same organs as the organs sitting here inside me – the bpNichol liver, the bpNichol kidney, the bladder, pancreas, b p – collected workings I think of as me. Which is why I worry if the Doctor knows me, my work, when I go in, worry that that Doctor may be a real collector, a completist. So you never ever say to the Doctor, 'Doctor, please save me.' No, you never say that. You say, 'what's wrong with me?' or 'I'm in rotten shape!' or, even better, 'I'm worthless!,' downplaying yourself, devaluing yourself, making yourself as miserable and undesirable as possible till the Doctor says, 'Collect yourself!' And you do. And he doesn't. Which is how you want things to be.

4 I almost got to meet my thyroid. I had been to see the Doctor and the Doctor said well it looked like my thyroid was enlarged and really I should get a thyroid scan and before you could say goiter there I was in this tiny room strapped down under this big machine & the

technician was saying not to worry because nothing bad was going to happen, I only had to lie there as still as possible for fifteen minutes or so and then I could get up and leave. So I lay there, as still as possible, thinking about my thyroid, thinking about leaving, my nose itching, my throat dry, lay there aware of my thyroid, tho I couldn't see it, even tho I couldn't see the technician who even then was looking at it, pictures of it, aware of my unseen thyroid, aware of the unseen technician who had so carefully left the room after she had strapped me down under the big machine, who had so carefully closed the lead-shielded doors and told me not to worry. And of course I worried. I always worry. Even tho you say you'd like to see it, you always worry when there's a chance you might finally get your wish, might finally see it, the unseen, might finally enter into that world, like turning inside out, a raw feeling. See? No, you don't want to see.

5 After I threw my back out I had more X-Rays, X-Rays of the lumbaar sacrum region. Only the Doctor that day was giving a lecture to these two trainees and as the technician shoved me around on the cold steel table he would whisper his commentaries. It was like those old TV game shows where the announcer would say 'what the studio audience doesn't know is,' and the trouble was I didn't know you see. You live your whole life making do with only the reflection of certain parts, making do with simply the names of your inner organs, their descriptions in books, while all around you are people who may actually have seen them, know directly what you only glimpse third-hand. Like your back. Every stranger on the street has had the chance to look at it but you only know it thru mirrors, photographs that other people take of you. And there are Doctors and Nurses who have cut you open, watched your blood flow, seen your heart pulse, know the inner man or woman. And these aren't just metaphors you know these aren't just similes. It is a discipline. We learn to see with the third eye, to listen with the third ear, to touch the unknown with the third hand, to walk down dark streets in search of the hidden, the unseen, while in the air around us invisible presences pick up their zithers and begin to play the *Third Man Theme.*

# love • zygal • art facts

Frame 2

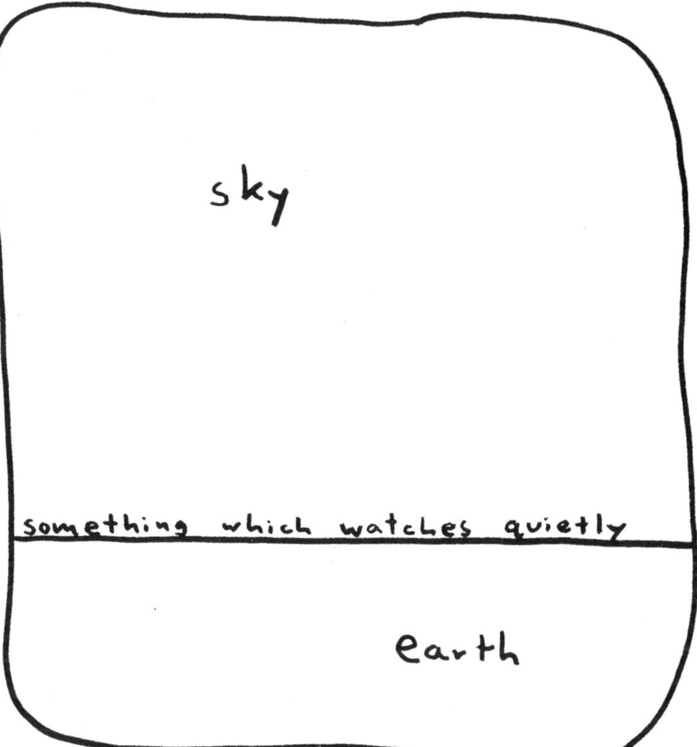


Frame 3

outside

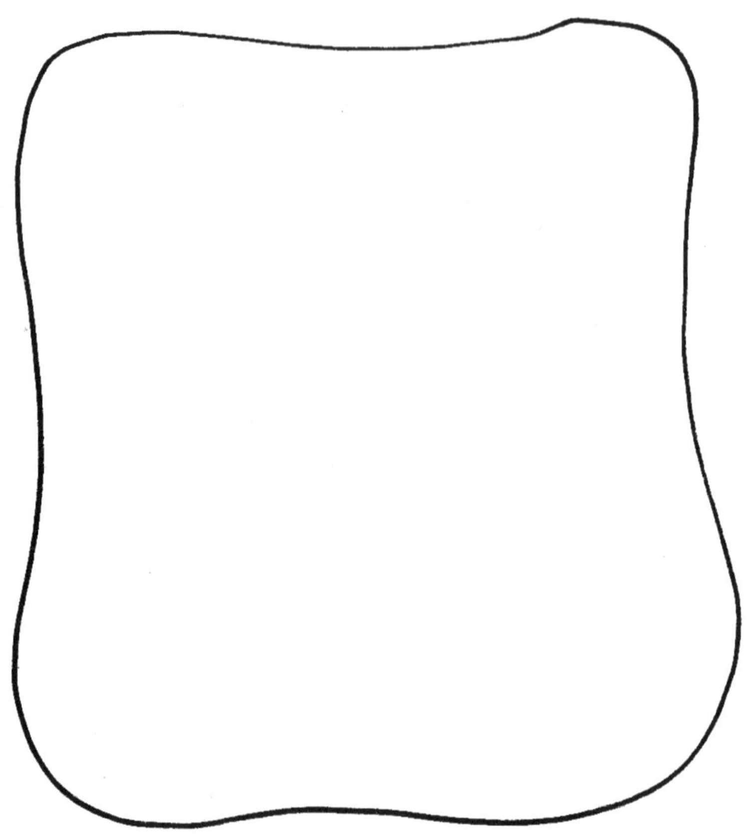

Frame 4

Frame 5

there is a sun setting

here there is a horizon

someone thinks

Frame 6

## Trans-Continental

1

an h moves past an m
an i becomes an r

someone throws a snowball

o p
t r s u
v v v

w

i i i i

2

x d

one mile

a sky which is grey
blue

do not serve yourself

l e
4 3 1 2 2

3

z

zero then nothing

3
6 9 10
13 5

here a z becomes an e
becomes an m a w

4

a d in a cloudbank
an r by a sea

perhaps it is a river
passes over

sky

sun

a town
in which the r becomes an l

5

a drainage ditch

an o

white white white
on a pole in a field
white white grey

two trees
three or four
est

ouest

est cinq est sept est
huite huite huite

6

this many miles from home
r becomes everything

s t t a p
z t m n n
o q l r
v s c d g

later there is hope
or lessness

perhaps you dream

t
v n h l p
z w a b

7

ness

ing

ch th sl le
e

a rocking motion
a creaking sound

an ack
a ly

8

crump cring
kasno alty

y

j a
t b

v t l m n q o p

b

b c d e g p
t v a j k l

l m n

m n o p

n o p a b
c d r f q

v
z
p

9

snow
s o o o
w n o s
n n n n

a white field
a green

(dark

darker than dark

est

a blue that is grey
an e

climbs up thru the cloudy sky
overwhelms me

10

j

r

k t o v m
l s me

you or i

we

11

up & down

wavey

w w w
w w w w

m
n u u n
m m

p

the sky turns greyer
turns erer

white & black

dark green

a t crossed by an h

resembles nothing more than
resembling

inging

rrrrrr

12

37-3

an h that is beyond me
turns brown
turns around

h or h

i then t

pause

39

today the weather is not fine
yesterday it was worse

152
nothing to do but dream
d g m v

13

snow at the window

white room

blue blue blue
blue blue blue
blue blue bluer

dark green & white
straight with branches
bending

g or h or

grey white grey
white grey white

wind

a sun which is hidden
a t in a snowbank

h h
h h

an I that insists itself
insists itself
insists

14

hornepayne to armstrong
h to a

ha!

ah ah ah ah

t
u v m l k
r s p

stops

s to s

bless this

15

a lake in a snowstorm
m's in clumps

o's & h's pile together

maybe an occasional a
perhaps a t

a sentence occurs
ending with the pronoun me

16

there is too much white
too many h's

life holds too much s or m
t b j f
m t

t's pile-up on t's
r's are scattered

an s lies broken in
the corner of
this room

17

a y by a road
a lake or a sea

wheat wheat wheat
brown among white

a fence
a fancy fold
a hill

i r k

a lady

light light light

18

a right a left
a flat latitude
fat laugh

a t h or e

here a longer line erupts suddenly

my toes are pointed west
my heels are pointed east

c

19

d b f g e
r z t l m
o o p d q b
l o c d k r n

y

t v z q p
l o r i k

b o m q l
l b c d y
j f
r t
m p h i i y t

20

empty eyes
empty skies
z z y

y x x w
w v v
u u t t s
s

bless this
i did say
yes yes yes
i did say i did say
bless this yes
bless this yes
bless yes yes

21

three deer
a field

a road that ends where h begins

two t's again

a w
a q
an ordinary o

later a z
a p

a field where horses pissed
yellow yellow

22

trees that are white not brown
with snow falling down

a footprint
an a

everything rises

a circle
a stadium
a town

a place where the road is brown not white

voices i cannot hear

h e l

wainwright

23

now there is a mountain
big not small
dark not light

soon there is a sun setting
a green tree
a memory of a time not now
h gone brown
falling to a c

d rises
r sets

the sooner the l
the later it gets

24

4
3 in a row
0 1 2

l t q r
farther than f
g

c d c d
l m n o
l m n o
p

repeated

not forseen

dreams
in which the dreamer dreams a dreamer
dreams a dreamer
dreams a dreamer
dreaming

25

m m m
an n which slants
disappears in o

u w u
m m m n
u v
o

grey sky
i wonder why

tear blue like you

c o k
j r
    j u

26

if there is lack of light is there no light

lack is black
height is white

why is h always h

now it is i
now t

z y x b
r v m n l

hello

yesterday i had a dream

last night i slept with the blind up

u t m d
l l
l

27

o dreaming
l sets

r rises black
blue blue blue

even the white turns green
purple
       black

black black black
back to blue

e rises

no

e does not rise
it is a dream

somewhere on this train
ryme schemes

28

g in a station
going white

wheat in a pool
number 8

7

a line that doesn't fit

6 in a row

g

29

more music
less o

balance

a pair of opposites that don't attract

t

a height of m
a weight of b
of a &

do i know you?
no!

a z or a p or an f

30

just another just another

broken heart
half-hearted dream

just another h another h another t

31

ing
inger

ongoing
undone

a voice that is soft is h or r

accent

a book that is full is empty

l z j q
g f g

(unfinished

another voice

m s
a b d

no choice of z)

32

e's in a cloud
voices that distract
e or e or e

f g a d l m k
r s o b j i

a distant v
a hum

a lady who is glum is sad

things ain't so bad

r

n or p

33

eyes in the dark
red not white

a starting point that is not right

an observation in a train station
a standing around

an h left lying on the ground

34

m
m z t p q
l y r k k k
j a h i w

o p d a
l b m z i
h r j r

is that right?
yes it fits

a narrow i
a thin t
an n that disappears

an m
an l
a g

35

a fantasy that fails to erupt
a disappointment

a sad pup
a happy kitten

two children asleep in the same bunk

an h by an m
an i by a t

here there is a vision

a choir sings

alleleuia
alleleuia
alleleuia

36

a longing for flesh
a flash of long

a lingering look
a languid mood

an l in a pool of pepsi

a cola
an a

(thinks)

something stops
something begins

rocking
l to m
nothing in between

is z is v is q is d

z to a

l d h z q t j

37

dark where there should be light

hot pants
cold thots

an r ringed in mist
later an s
then a t

if only the moon came up
the I would rise

settles on my shoulders

mood

38

a trance state
a continental trance

je ne sais pas monsieur
je ne sais pas madame

hello in the morning
goodbye in the afternoon

it has been h or w knowing you
y or m

it has been z
t u v l k
j r j

39

a face above a mountain
an m above a c

l j r u p k
m s z y v b d

i already said that

it is a snow cloud
an f day
a q g r

a fish in a river too cold to swim in

an absence of crowds

40

a saint
a gesture in the sky

an m on a mountaintop
a sequence of o's

a catalogue
a heaven
a vision of vision

h i r m
s t
l q

41

a new beginning
an ending

a slowing down
a speeding up

an arc in a park
an f in a rainstorm

2's or 3's
4 5 7

a leaning back
a falling forward

tree stumps

42

a needle
a fir
an e

l y j k m n
o z w u
v t m n n
k s l

sing ing

a bell on a breast
a blessed beast
bust

j or h
k or m

43

hair that is blonde is long

a dirty hand

a land that is lost
forgotten

a little girl that's frightened

a mood of g
a presence of m

l k
r s y t n

44

an ending a beginning
a beginning to see an end

a line that extends then collapses

a lax breath
he lacks it

a tree by a track
a rack & a scream

a tension
a lack of it
a lick

a lucky strike
a struck lock

an a that can't pretend

45

is this the end
it is not the end
we will say it is the end

a g k or l
m t z y v
w w
u u
l k r p p
d o k j r

the sun is up
the sky is blue

look at the grey clouds

i see them

y y y y
y y y

46

a b c d
f g e i
j j j j j
k l m
k l m
n o
    p

a c o or n
q v z w p
t t y a
b x u

47

green & red
black among white

a lighter sky
a darker hill

a u or z

narrow

thin but long

t p j l

48

a sand bar
an old car

a chocolate
a noise

t p l m n
o o o

a road by a track
a toad on a back 40

3 or 2
one e f

bridge

truck

sky eye

49

final finale
definite end end

h w w t
hope now awful hat

here
h e r e

heir & hair
or hare air

weir

wierdly y & d
j k k
g t

toronto - vancouver
march 13 - 16        1971

## Allegories

Allegory #1

Allegory # 4

Allegory #6

Allegory #8

Allegory #11

Allegory #22

Allegory #29

Allegory # 30

**song for saint ein**

i look at you this way

noun then verb

these are my words

i sing to you

*

no separation no

the same thing

i am these words
these words say so

somewhere i exist separate from this page
this cage of sounds & signs

i am this noise

my voice says so

## Self-contradiction

*december 72*

abcdefghijklmNO

**probable systems 8**

given
prose
~~poetry~~ x 3 = H

&

poetry
~~prose~~ ÷ 3= I

then
prose = ⅓H & poetry = 3I

since H = 8 & I = 9
then
prose = 2⅔ & poetry = 27

BUT
since poetry – (oetry) + (rose) = prose
& since o = 15 e = 5 t = 20 r = 18 y = 25 & s = 19
then 27 – 83 + 57 = 2⅔
& 1 = 2⅔

similarly: prose – rose + oetry = 27
yielding 2⅔ – 57 + 83 = 27
or 28⅔ = 27

subtracting the smaller # from the larger # in both of the above cases we arrive at a value of 1⅔ the measured difference between prose & poetry

*commentary:*

another way of figuring arrives at a different answer since poetry = 99 & prose = 73 then the difference between them is 26 or the number of letters in the alphabet  since this method appears more precise what is the value of the first answer arrived at

starting from the basic premise that H & I follow one another in the alphabet having a different value of 1 (poetry & prose placed in the same base have a difference of 10)  the relationship between them is perfect  by turning I one counter clock-wise position it becomes H  by turning H one counter clock-wise position it becomes I (C&U M&W N&Z are the only other letters whose relationships to one another are at all similar  however none of these is as perfect in relation to one another as H&I)  in the premise the fractioning or multiplying of poetry & prose by 3 (the number of the mother continent MU (MUse?)) is an expression in mathematical terms of the effect of cosmic forces on the writing  (the initial relationship is demonstrated by the transforming of poetry into prose using the alphabetic replacement system prior to multiplying & then the reverse prior to dividing  prose is multiplied by 3 because the cosmic forces are less present in prose since the consciousness of the writer tends to intrude to a much greater degree  thus to equalize the equalizable factors as much as possible poetry is subsequently divided by 3)  since the relationship between H&I is the closest approximation in pure language terms of the relationship between poetry & prose by using them as equivalents we arrive at a purer mathematical description  both answers are right  26 comes closest to the traditional english grammar ideal  1⅔ is purer because it brings into play the flux in the world of the writer & its relationship to writing  it is interesting to note that the value of 1 is a multiple of 3 thus arriving at 27 as the value of poetry as opposed to ⅜ as the value of prose  note the simplicity & directness of the relationship between poetry & the cosmic forces  further to this in the final transformation in both cases 1⅔ is actually an expression of the margin of difference in transformational writing i.e. when one is moving from poetry into prose or vice versa  this is to say that 1⅔ is a measure of their difference in terms of borderblur writing as opposed to (as is the case with 26) an expression of their gross difference if you do not try bringing the two things together  1⅔ is an expression of the degree of flux in actual transformational writing

**Pastoral**

*for Mike Ondaatje*

*summer 73*

**love song**
*for Margaret Avison*

the le the the an a année annie saint ani slaus    that that or
this this    what what asked    the's in confusion    some
a's    a train passes thru    or an or    an an    standing    &
after sitting standing    (yesterday this would've been different
tomorrow it will not be the same)    & after standing sitting
after sitting sitting    not sitting    & then you came

**love song 3**

when there are no roles left
when he has finally come
back to the fearful point he had fled from
where all pain & futility he has felt dwells
knowing the hell she knelt in
& yet gave birth
                                        he is torn between praise & scorn
the wanting that has screamed inside him
afraid to face again
the emptiness he felt calling her name
in a darkened room the mind inhabits as its own
knowing the love he felt for her she could never return
burned up by the passion of her own dead desires
no life for the living form crawled out of her
who still, today, moves under the sway of that hunger
will not be consoled
no matter what arms he finds to hold him
what nipples his mouth closes round
because he is older & the wanting will not make it so

## three small songs for gladys hindmarch

language is or was or has been has been said before i did say once as gertrude did commas are disgusting little things such sucks she did did not say said they do things for you you should do for yourself they make you lazy    ruling out commas what did i say was it yesterday or the day before sitting on this plane drunk there is this nun behind this guy is badgering says he knows something about her he will tell her later but he knows her    late or early sitting up i'm tired no well okay this one time son sure you can stay up & listen to the radio    tomorrow i'll step off to continue as words or language does that sense of it continually run together in our heads articulate the causal separations    when the baby comes the silver spoon screaming from the mouth we are blessed    all that is best & wonderful

★

up is down
as down is up

a cradle & a rug in a rain storm

a g & an f
an r of seeing you
being with you
m & p

hot tumble heart pin
just best can't chin show
loving & knowing
stumble

speech is speech is speech

a pumpkin &
a tunnel a
tornado

★

images imagine packages this is the way it is    yesterday the wind blew today the sky is blue    if the wind blows does the sky blow

this is a story i mentioned before imagine the imagination can you    this is how you begin    the image is imagination    dear gladys    today the sky is without form it is colour only or imagine how the sky's form is imaginary (it is) as saint ory told me that was a different story i could not imagine then

scene: a small window completely filled with blue    the action is from left to right    imagine someone walks thru    a saint addresses you

this is the way i sing my song    this is the way you write the tune    imagine imagining imagining can you

## probable systems

*thot probes for rob   late january 1970*

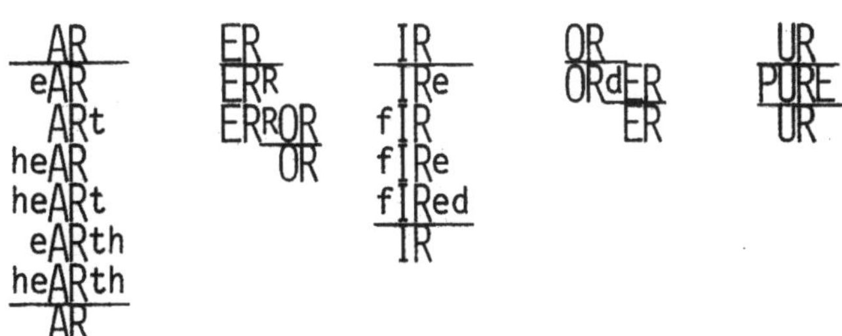

## probable systems 15

*division of the signified*

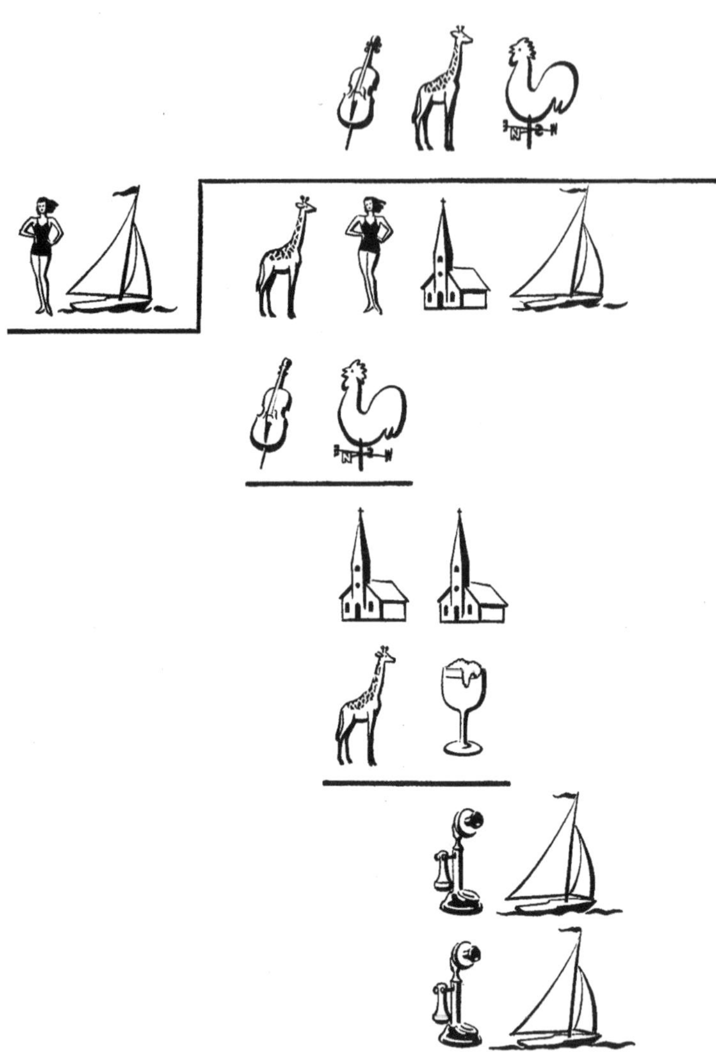

## The Frog Variations

*for Louise Prael*

1 Dawn fog  
log  
bog

Noon frog  
log  
bog

Dusk fog  
frog  
bog

2 fog fog fog frog fog

3 moonfrog  
pondfrog  
frogfrog

4 (definition of a lily-pad)  
fragile  
frog île

5 (the frog's obsession with the fly)  
frog'll oggle all

6 frog's tongue: fly catcher  
frog's eye: bird measure  
frog stung  
frog sigh  
bird fly

7 o moon
no moon

o frog
no frog

o pond
no pond

o
no

o
no

o
no

8 splash

splayed beneath the bending ash
fragile children of the great bog
frog

pond

poised under the autumn frond
more singers of the dark water croon
moon

9 into the sky at night
the moon & all her frogs drop

under the brilliant light of the pond
rippling life goes on

bpNichol
July 10th, 1981
'one of the Basho Street Kids'

**Three Months in New York City**
*The Actual Life of Language 1*

CARTER

FIRE
SNOW

MINERS
CARTER
QUEENS

COURT
UNIONS

BEGIN
ISRAELI
ISRAELIS
KIDNAP
OK

BARE

ISRAEL
PEACE
FEAR
DRIVE

ISRAELI

BEGIN
STEEL
CARTER
4

ARRAIGN
STRIKE
REPORT
'BUNNIES'
NURSING

COP
SCHOOL
HOLD
'DEAD'
LOCAL
HINT

HOW
WALL
SENATE
TRACE
SENATE
SPINKS

EX-DRUG
SAM
I
FORT
51
PROBE

2
BOOK
KIDNAPED
SUN
2
BERKOWITZ

OIL
SON
MORO
AGREE
CARTER

HEAVY
PATTY
ORDER
RESCUE
LBJ

SICK
BERKOWITZ
JOE
HUNT
CARTER
PORT

RIDERS
MUST
A

*New York Daily News*
1978

## Sixteen Lilypads

| | | | |
|---|---|---|---|
| frog | fro? | fr?g | ?rog |
| f?og | ?r?g | ??og | f?o? |
| ?ro? | fr?? | f??g | ???g |
| f??? | ??o? | ?r?? | ???? |

```
           asea ease  ease
          ease seas  seas
         seas asea  asea
        asea ease  ease
       ease seas  seas
      seas asea  asea
       easease  ease
        aseas  seas
        aseas asea
       easeasease
      seas aseas
     asea  aseas
    ease  easease
   seas  seas asea
  asea    ease seas
 ease      asea ease
seas        seas asea
 ease        ease seas
  asea       seas  ease
   seas    asea     asea
    ease  ease       seas
     aseaseas         ease
      seasea         seas
       ease         asea
        as         ease
                  seas
                 asea
                ease
```

**Catching Frogs**
*for LeRoy Gorman*

jar din

fr

pond

glop

## Water Poem 5

**probable systems 24**
*physical contexts of human words*

In a number of the preceding PROBABLE SYSTEMS, we have been examining concepts like 'the weight of speech,' 'the speed of thot,' etc. What becomes increasingly apparent is the need for certain world standards when it comes to print. Something as simple as measuring the circumference of words is made meaningless by the virtual babel of type-faces and type-sizes.

If a world standard were adopted – something like, say, 10 pt, or 12 pt, Helvetica, Garamond or Futura – then numerous variables could be taken into account & meaningful discussions & research could begin to take place. For instance, a more accurate notation of pitch and volume variables would become possible.* It could also illuminate discussion of the justified paragraph versus the preferred typographic mode of ragged right. And, of course, that old question of the time it takes for the mind to get around certain old thinking would finally be answerable.

This is merely to point to the advantages of setting up such a standard. Those interested could begin by forming local study groups to discuss the problem and approaches to be taken in order to get their government to adopt the notion of a World Standard for Print Size & Style. We can only hope that this initiative does not go the way of Esperanto.

written: Spring 1978
additional research & final draft: Summer 1988

---

*As an instance of what i'm saying here: pitch could be tracked through gradated use of type-faces; similarly, volume could be indicated by gradated use of type-sizes.

## Before Closure

*1965/66?*

a closet closes. a close loss seen
becomes a loss enacted. all loss seems active
(closest to the heart). closure means
a loss of becoming
becomes
a closet in ourselves
closing.

# afterword

**This book is a frame.**

You can see bpNichol's work through it, but our frame, like many frames, has glass in it – glass that colours and textures, reduces and magnifies, reflects, refracts and, yes, occasionally distorts. Any book that pretends to do otherwise can be trusted even less than usual.

*The Alphabet Game* is indeed 'a' reader. Given bpNichol's extraordinary literary output, what we present here is by necessity only a fraction of what he wrote in his lifetime; there have been, and we hope there will be, other collections of his work, in both print and digital form. This is only the beginning, again.

While we have tried to include exemplary or representative texts from the whole of Nichol's writing career, slipping in a few of our favourites here and there, nearly all of the texts in *The Alphabet Game* were written as parts of longer series. We would like to point out that we have had to remove these works from their textual conditions – not only from the context of the longer series themselves, but also from the particularity of their original typefaces, dimensions on the page, adjacency to other texts, bindings, type of paper, etc. In presenting these selections in a volume with a standardized format, we have changed the meanings of these texts even further. Still, we hope that we are providing readers with a lens that will allow a closer examination of the shapes and contours of Nichol's writing. It is our belief that from here, readers will feel moved to look at, touch, read the originals available from artists and bookmakers, bookstores, library archives and various digital archival projects.

Selecting excerpts from the nine books of *The Martyrology* proved to be particularly and excruciatingly difficult. Aside from problems inherent to pulling out passages from a continuous, lifelong work, the question arose: which *Martyrology* do we present? Or, whose *Martyrology*? We tried to include some continuous series (such as 'Continental Trance' from *The Martyrology Book 6 Books*), especially those with thematic or formal strains that run through the whole collection. We also relied heavily on recommendations for excerpts from those who teach and study Nichol's work. We are very grateful for the suggestions we received, as this reader as a whole represents a successful collaborative effort. Again, we trust that the open-ended strains in the excerpts from *The Martyrology* (for example, in the chains in *Book 5*) will compel readers to seek out the whole text in its original form.

Finally, although there is an extraordinary embarrassment of riches of available bpNichol material (much of which is in the Simon Fraser University archives), we have largely limited this collection to non-commercial work published during Nichol's lifetime, excluding, for example, Nichol's writing for the children's television show *Fraggle Rock*. Since the companion website to this book at bpnichol.ca will present high-quality colour images and sound files, we also have chosen not to include photographs of Nichol's poetic objects or a CD of his sound work in this collection. We have excluded one other large body of work from this collection; even though Nichol was committed to collaboration, working with the sound poetry ensemble The Four Horsemen, with Steve McCaffery as part of the Toronto Research Group, with the visual artist Barbara Caruso, and with countless other writers and artists, we have decided to spotlight Nichol's solo ventures. For those who may be willing to take up the editorial challenge, there is more than enough collaborative material to produce another entire volume …

In the meantime, we have established a website, bpnichol.ca, which will continue the project that *The Alphabet Game* has begun, acting as an open-ended online anthology. The site will house a range of digitized Nichol material, including sound files of Nichol's recordings, full-colour images and scans of his musical scores. Our goal is simple: to ensure that as much of Nichol's work as possible stays available in as many forms as possible. To paraphrase Nichol, there are infinite alphabets ahead.

Lori Emerson & Darren Wershler-Henry
September 2007

## Notes on the Poems

Nichol's print work demonstrates a particular and exacting commitment to the materiality of the printed page. Throughout his life, he published in the widest imaginable variety of forms: stapled collections of typescript; handwritten, folded mimeo pamphlets; finely typeset perfect-bound books making use of particular paper stock, ink colours and typefaces; boxed collections of loose sheets of a variety of sizes; and objects made of cardstock and thread, to name only a few.

Attempting to fit such a heterogeneity into the framework of any book becomes what Nichol referred to in his own practice as translation. Translation never produces an exact equivalence, not only because of linguistic differences, but also because the experience of the reader differs from edition to edition – poems published in different forms look, feel, and even smell differently. Meanings inevitably shift as texts are packed into a new context.

These brief comments describe some of the editorial and design decisions that we made when assembling this collection. Unless the notes indicate otherwise, all digital reproductions appear at the original scale. A brief bibliography follows.

★

The version of 'The Complete Works' that begins this volume is a scanned reproduction of Nichol's small-press version from GANGLIA's New Mimeos (#5): a folded piece of blue cardstock with the title on the outside and the typed poem within.

The first two editions of *Konfessions of an Elizabethan Fan Dancer* were typescripts, designed and published by Bob Cobbing (Writer's Forum) and Nelson Ball (Weed/Flower Press) respectively. The third (like the second, edited by Nelson Ball, but designed by damian lopes and published by Coach House) is a careful, desktop-published simulation of a typescript. As the latter is still in print, we decided to present reduced reproductions (at 75% of the original size) of pages from the second edition, published by Nelson Ball in 1973.

'Dada Lama' (a work that is as much a sound poem score as it is a concrete poem) appears here in a slightly modified version of a typeface called Monospace 821. We have used this face throughout the book for poems that, like Nichol's typescripts, partially depend on vertical alignment to achieve various literary effects, but have previously been published in proportionally spaced typefaces (such as the versions in both of the two previous volumes of Nichol's selected works), which compromised some of those effects. The tradeoff is that Monospace 821 also has a distinct personality which brings new connotations to the piece, so while this version allows for a wider range of literary effects than a proportionally spaced version, it is no way 'closer' to an 'original.'

'untitled [nnnnnn]' is a Nichol piece from *The Cosmic Chef*, a boxed set of concrete poetry edited by Nichol and published by Oberon Press in 1970. This piece is unusual in Nichol's typewritten concrete because of its use of masking and cut-out techniques. It is reproduced at 75% size.

*Still Water* was published as a boxed set of loose, unnumbered 5" by 5" cards, so the order of the poems excerpted here is somewhat arbitrary. The frame on each page represents the trim size of the original card. Like the originals, these versions of the poems have been set in Univers, though the move to a computer typeface has created a greater degree of uniformity here than is found in the originals.

*ABC: The Aleph Beth Book* was commercially printed in a 6" by 6" format, with red hairline borders around each glyph. The images here include the fragments of the typed manifesto that appeared on each page in the original edition.

The images in this collection from *Aleph Unit* are reproduced from Barbara Caruso's hand-cut silkscreen versions.

'H (an alphhabet)' from *Alphhabet Ilphabet*, was drawn by Barbara Caruso and published by her Seripress in 1978.

The selections in this collection from *The Martyrology* presented us with particular challenges. First off, extracting anything from a work that ran to six thick volumes in Nichol's lifetime and posthumously expanded to nine volumes precludes the possibility of anything like a representative sampling. Fortunately, the whole *Martyrology* remains in print, so what we offer here is utterly and unabashedly subjective. We are especially grateful to David Rosenberg for his aid in making these selections.

In the layout and design of *The Martyrology,* Nichol employed very long lines set very closely together. Moreover, he used the page as a unit of composition. With the exception of our inclusion of page numbers and section titles, we have maintained Nichol's line length, spacing, page length and page positioning for these pieces, though in instances where a section begins or ends mid-page, the text preceding or following it has been omitted. An ellipsis [...] in the margins represents where an excerpt begins and ends. Third, though we have included reproductions of Jerry Ofo's drawings in this edition, we have not duplicated the coloured ink, which is particularly important to the purple pages of the first three books of *The Martyrology*.

'Part 1' and 'Part 3' are excerpts from *Journeying & the Returns*, a book of poetry that was included in the box *bp* along with the loose visual poems in the *Letters Home* envelope, the flip book *Wild Thing*, and the record *borders*. 'Statement' was printed on the back of the *bp* box.

The poems in this collection from *Translating Translating Apollinaire* fall into two broad groups: those that have been typeset and those that appear as 75% scale reproductions of the typescript. The former do not depend in any significant way on physical layout or monospacing.

Despite the claim that the very title of *Two Novels* makes to being prose, it makes very particular usage of line length, line breaks and other poetic effects. Moreover, it was illustrated (in the first edition, you had to stick the illustrations in place yourself), and the illustrations were in colour. To complicate things further, the book was modelled after the old Ace SF double editions: when you finished reading one book, you could flip it over, and where the back cover would be on a normal book, the second book began. Both books ended in the middle of the single volume. And, for some reason, the page lengths differ in the hardcover and paperback editions. The layout in this volume preserves the page length, line breaks and line lengths of the hardcover edition, and includes in-line versions of the original illustrations, with the deliberately poor-quality coloured (or murky grey) halftone screening removed. In other words, the version of

*Andy* you see here (like much of the rest of this book) is a digital diagram of an object that never existed in this form.

The excerpts from *Craft Dinner* in this volume are also prose or prose poetry, but they maintain all of the original Aya Press edition's line breaks.

The section of Nichol's powerful prose poem *Journal* that appears in this book maintains the original line breaks, and it attempts to replicate the spacing, to the extent that that is possible to do so in a different typeface.

'Trans-Continental,' like 'Dada Lama,' depends on vertical spacing for some of its meaning effects, and was originally published in a proportionally spaced font. It has been reset here in modified Monospace 821. All line lengths and page lengths are Nichol's.

The images in 'Alegories' appear here at 75% of their published size.

'Sixteen Lilypads,' 'untitled [asea/ease]' and 'Catching Frogs' have been set in modified Monospace 821 for the same reasons that the typeface was employed elsewhere in this book.

## Select Bibliography

This is a chronological list of works by bpNichol, including those we have excerpted in this reader as well as other major publications. We suggest that readers seek out John Curry's (jwcurry's) astonishing, exhaustive, ongoing 'beepliography' of all Nichol's published writings. Readers may also wish to consult the bibliographies in Douglas Barbour's *bpNichol and His Works* (ECW Press, 1991), Stephen Scobie's *bpNichol: What History Teaches* (Talonbooks, 1984) or the list of Nichol's visual work in Gil McElroy's *St. Art: The Visual Poetry of bpNichol* (Confederation Centre Art Gallery & Museum, 2000). Also note that, while long out of print, many of Nichol's recordings listed below are available from the online audio archive PennSound: <writing.upenn.edu/pennsound/x/Nichol.html>

### Print Works

*Cycles Etc.* Cleveland: 7 Flowers Press, 1965.

*Scraptures: Second Sequence.* Toronto: GANGLIA, 1965.

*bp.* Box includes *Journeying & the Returns* (book), *Letters Home* (an envelope of loose visual poems), *borders* (record), *Wild Thing* (flip book) and 'Statement' printed on the back of the box. Toronto: Coach House Press, 1967.

*Konfessions of an Elizabethan Fan Dancer.* London, UK: Writer's Forum, 1967. Rev. ed. Toronto: Weed/Flower Press, 1973. Rev. ed. with an introduction by Nelson Ball, Toronto: Coach House Books, 2004.

*Ballads of the Restless Are.* Sacramento: Runcible Spoon, 1968.

*The Complete Works.* Toronto: GANGLIA, 1968.

*Two Novels.* Includes *Andy* and *For Jesus Lunatick.* Toronto: Coach House Press, 1969. Rev. ed. 1971.

*The Cosmic Chef: An Evening of Concrete.* Ed. bpNichol. Ottawa: Oberon Press, 1970.

*Beach Head.* Transitions 66/67. Sacramento: Runcible Spoon, 1970.

*The True Eventual Story of Billy the Kid*. Toronto: Weed/Flower Press, 1970.

*Still Water*. Vancouver: Talon Books, 1970.

*ABC: the aleph beth book*. Ottawa: Oberon Press, 1971.

*The Other Side of the Room*. Toronto: Weed/Flower Press, 1971.

*The Captain Poetry Poems*. Vancouver: blewointmentpress, 1971.

*Monotones*. Vancouver: Talon Books, 1971.

*The Martyrology Books 1 & 2*. Toronto: Coach House Press, 1972. Rev. ed. 1977. Coach House Books, 1997.

*The Adventures of Milt the Morph in Colour*. With Barbara Caruso. Toronto: Seripress, 1972.

*Aleph Unit*. Toronto: Seripress, 1973.

*love: a book of remembrances*. Vancouver: Talon Books, 1974.

*The Martyrology Books 3 & 4*. Toronto: Coach House Press, 1976. Coach House Books, 2000.

*Alphhabet Ilphabet*. Toronto: Seripress, 1978.

*From My Window*. Toronto: Seripress, 1978.

*Journal*. Toronto: Coach House Press, 1978.

*Craft Dinner: Stories & Texts, 1966–1976*. Toronto: Aya Press, 1978.

*Translating Translating Apollinaire: A Preliminary Report from A Book of Research*. Milwaukee: Membrane Press, 1979.

*In England Now That Spring*. With Steve McCaffery. Toronto: Aya Press, 1979.

*As Elected: Selected Writing 1962–1979*. Ed. bpNichol and Jack David. Vancouver: Talon Books, 1980.

*Briefly*. Lantzville: Island Writing Series, 1981.

*Extreme Positions*. Edmonton: Longspoon Press, 1981.

*The Martyrology Book 5*. Toronto: Coach House Press, 1982. Coach House Books, 2006.

*The Frog Variations*. Toronto: curvd H&z, 1982.

*Once: A Lullaby*. With Ed Roach. Windsor: Black Moss Press, 1983.

*Continental Trance*. Lantzville: Oolichan Books, 1983.

*Still*. Vancouver: Pulp Press, 1983.

*To the End of the Block*. Windsor: Black Moss Press, 1984.

*Giants, Moosequakes & Other Disasters*. Windsor: Black Moss Press, 1985.

*zygal: a book of mysteries & translations*. Toronto: Coach House Press, 1986. Coach House Books, 2000.

*You Too, Nicky*. Vancouver: Fissure, 1986.

*The Martyrology Book 6 Books*. Toronto: Coach House Press, 1987.

*Selected Organs: Parts of an Autobiography*. Windsor: Black Moss Press, 1988.

*Bored Messengers*. Prince george: Gorse Press, 1988.

*art facts: a book of contexts*. Tucson: Chax Press, 1990.

*Gifts: The Martyrology Book(s) 7 &*. Music: Howard Gerhard. Toronto: Coach House Press, 1990. Coach House Books, 2003.

*Rational Geomancy: The Kids of the Book-Machine/The Collected Research Reports of the Toronto Research Group 1973–1982*. With Steve McCaffery. Vancouver: Talon Books, 1992.

*Ad Sanctos: The Martyrology Book 9*. Toronto: Coach House Press, 1993.

*First Screening*. Toronto: Underwhich Editions, 1984. Red Deer: Red Deer College Press, 1993. Prepared for the web <www.vispo.com/bp/> by Jim Andrews, Geof Huth, Lionel Kearns, Marko Niemi and Dan Waber, 2007.

*truth: a book of fictions*. Ed. Irene Niechoda. Stratford: Mercury Press, 1993.

*Back Lane Letters*. Toronto: Letters, 1984.

*An H in the Heart: A Reader*. Eds. George Bowering, Michael Ondaatje and Stan Dragland. Toronto: McClelland & Stewart Inc., 1994.

*HOLIDAY*. Ottawa: curvd H&z 443, 1999.

**Recordings**

*Motherlove*. Toronto: Allied Records, 1968.

*bpNichol*. bpNichol. Toronto: High Barnet, 1971.

*Ear Rational*. Milwaukee: Membrane Press, 1982.

**Films**

*Sons of Captain Poetry*. Dir. Michael Ondaatje. Toronto: Mongrel Films, 1970.

*bp: Pushing the Boundaries*. Dir. Brian Nash. Toronto: CINéMAT, 1998.

## Permissions

Poems from *Konfessions of An Elizabethan Fan Dancer* (1973) and *The Other Side of the Room* (1971) reproduced by permission of Weed/Flower Press.

'Dada Lama' and 'Two Words: A Wedding' reprinted from *As Elected: Selected Writing 1962–1979* (1980) by permission of Talon Books.

Poems from *Still Water* (1970) reprinted by permission of Talon Books.

'Manifesto,' 'A,' 'B,' 'C,' 'D,' 'E,' 'F,' 'H,' 'I,' 'J,' 'K' and 'L' from *ABC: The Aleph Beth Book* are reprinted by permission of Oberon Press.

Poems from *Aleph Unit* (1973) and 'H (an alphhabet)' from *Alphabet Ilphabet* (1978), are reproduced by permission of Seripress.

Excerpts from *The Martyrology*, *Journeying & the Returns*, *Two Novels*, *Journal* and *zygal* reproduced by permission of Coach House Books.

Poems from *Translating Translating Apollinaire* reproduced by permission of Membrane Press, Milwaukee, 1979. Much of the book, along with its sequel and related work, appear online:
<www.thing.net/~grist/l&d/bpnichol/bp.htm>

Section 4 from *Extreme Positions* reprinted by permission (Edmonton: Longspoon Press, 1981).

Poems from *Craft Dinner* reproduced by permission of Aya Press (later The Mercury Press, 1978).

Excerpt from *Still* reprinted by permission of Arsenal Pulp Press.

Poems from *Selected Organs* reprinted by permission of Black Moss Press.

Poems from *love: a book of remembrances* (1974) reprinted by permission of Talon Books.

Thanks to Ellie Nichol and Chax Press for permission to reprint 'The Frog Variations,' 'Three Months in New York City,' 'Sixteen Lilypads,' ‘probable systems 19,’ ‘[asea/ease]’ ‘Catching Frogs,’ ‘fr/pond/glop,’ ‘probable systems 24’ and ‘Water Poem 5,’ which first appeared in *art facts: a book of contexts* (Tucson: Chax Press, 1990).

‘Before Closure’ reproduced by permission from *truth: a book of fictions* (Toronto: The Mercury Press, 1993).

All other works reprinted by permission of Ellie Nichol on behalf of the bpNichol estate.

## Index of Poem and Book Titles

**Acknowledgements**

Many people were involved in the production of this book.

Thanks, as usual, to everyone at Coach House (Stan Bevington, Alana Wilcox, Rick/Simon, Christina Palassio, Evan Munday, John De Jesus, Nicky Drumbolis, Tony Glenesk, John Barbeito, Orlan Barnett-Jang, Ron McAlpin) for continuing to make improbable books like this one possible. Special thanks to Sarah Hipworth for patiently and thoroughly assembling all of the myriad bits and pieces that went into this collection – this book would not exist without her hard work.

Thanks to Ellie Nichol for the idea for this book in the first place, and for all the help along the way. Thanks to Smaro Kamboureli, who was part of the inception of this project and guided its subsequent development.

Thanks to Justin Stephenson for taking Nichol into the third dimension with his amazing cover design.

Thanks to the many people we consulted while assembling this text, especially those who took the time to offer valuable feedback, to aid in the location of originals, to scan and photocopy work and generally to behave in a generous and heroic manner: Nelson Ball, Doug Barbour, derek beaulieu, Christian Bök, George ('can kick your dad's ass') Bowering, Barbara Caruso, jwcurry, Beverley Daurio, Frank Davey, Jack David, Nicky Drumbolis, Paul Dutton, Mark Fram, Michael Holmes, damian lopes, Karen Mac Cormack, Steve McCaffery, Michael Ondaatje, a. rawlings, Karl Siegler, Steven Scobie, Lola Tostevin.

Epic thanks to David Rosenberg for the time he spent making suggestions for selections from *The Martyrology*.

bpNichol (Barrie Phillip Nichol) was born September 30, 1944, in Vancouver, British Columbia. He died in Toronto, Ontario, on September 25, 1988.

Nichol's writing is, by definition, engaged with a phenomenon he called 'borderblur': in his lifetime he wrote (somewhere between) poetry, novels, short fiction, children's books, musical scores, comic book art, collage/assemblage and computer texts. Nichol was also an inveterate collaborator, working with the sound poetry ensemble The Four Horsemen (Nichol, Rafael Barreto-Rivera, Paul Dutton and Steve McCaffery); with Steve McCaffery as part of the Toronto Research Group (TRG); with the visual artist Barbara Caruso; and with countless other writers.

Nichol also had (and continues to have) a large presence on screens of various sizes. In the mid-1980s, he became a writer for the children's television show *Fraggle Rock*, produced by Jim Henson. His early work in sound was documented in Michael Ondaatje's short film *Sons of Captain Poetry*. A second full-length film on Nichol, *bp: pushing the boundaries*, directed by Brian Nash, was completed in the 1990s. Nichol also appears in Ron Mann's film *Poetry in Motion*.

Though Nichol's initial attempts at writing in the early 1960s produced fiction and lyric poetry, he first garnered international attention with his hand-drawn concrete and visual poems. These texts work brilliantly against the conventions of the traditional lyric poem by exploring the material, tangible and aural qualities of the word and the letter. (Not surprisingly, Nichol's work with the aural qualities of language led him to sound poetry, resulting in the release of four solo audio recordings.)

Nichol's first major collection of concrete poetry, *Konfessions of an Elizbethan Fan Dancer*, marked the beginning of a long engagement with the typewriter and its unique ability to mechanically reproduce letters an exact distance apart. In other words, the grid-like qualities of typewritten text allowed Nichol to create meaning semantically and horizontally as well as visually and vertically. Soon after, Nichol was boxing and publishing loose pages of concrete in *bp*, *Still Water* and an edited collection, *The Cosmic Chef: An Evening of Concrete*. While Nichol's concrete poems illustrate an astonishing range of techniques and concerns, other early works such as *ABC: the aleph beth book* and *Aleph Unit* point to his lifelong interest in representing process by gradually transforming series of letter-shapes.

Exemplifying the dictum spelled out in the 'Statement' printed on the back of *bp* that 'there are no barriers in art,' Nichol won the 1970 Governor General's Award for poetry with not one but four publications: the prose booklet *The True Eventual Story of Billy the Kid*, the collection of lyric poems *Beach Head*, the boxed concrete sequence *Still Water* and *The Cosmic Chef*, a boxed anthology of concrete and visual poetry.

It was partly through his work with concrete poetry in sequences such as the one in *Extreme Positions* that Nichol discovered innovative ways to work with narrative. Nichol reworked and remixed the conventions of the novel, the western, the detective story, the romance, the diary and the autobiography. The results included the deconstructive metafiction of *The True Eventual Story of Billy the Kid*; the mad jumble of prose poetry, seedy sexploitation, personal and historical letters, science fiction and cartoons that is *Two Novels*; the stream-of-consciousness of *Journal*; the autobiographical accounts of Nichol's vagina, tonsils, lungs and other vital bits in *Selected Organs*; and so on.

Nichol continued to subvert formal and thematic conventions in his shorter poems and sequences. He moved effortlessly between genres, blurring and experimenting with generic boundaries to produce writing as varied as the minimalist lyricism of *The Other Side of the Room*; the pun-filled, semantically complex *Journeying & the Returns*; the translations of translations of (who else?) Apollinaire in *Translating Translating Apollinaire*.

The series of books that began with *love: a book of remembrances* and was followed by *Zygal: A Book of Mysteries and Translations*, *art facts: a book of contexts*, and the posthumous *Truth: a book of fictions* was an ideal means for Nichol to continue developing a number of poem sequences. These range from his concrete letter poems to the series 'probable systems,' 'I.T.A.N.U.T.S.' and 'Studies in the Book Machine.' Most readers and critics see Nichol's *The Martyrology* not only as the culmination of all of his work but as one of the most important long poems of the twentieth century. Begun in 1967 and remaining unfinished at the time of his death in 1988, *The Martyrology* is an open-ended, lifelong poem that endlessly problematizes issues of textuality, reading and writing.

Given Nichol's dedication to the process of writing, it should come as no surprise that the form of *The Martyrology* underwent countless transformations over the years – writing, rewriting and expanding on previous books, formally and thematically inventing and reinventing itself and its pantheon of linguistic 'saints' (words beginning with the letters 'st') over and over again. For example, the section 'Clouds' from *Book 2*, which continues to explore the mythology of the saints first introduced in *Book 1*, is brought back as the ghostly presence of *Book 5*'s 'Chain 11' – Nichol has systematically taken out most of the words and left only clusters of certain letters. As Nichol said of *The Martyrology* in 1987, 'This text has not closed.'